D0079418

CREATING AND SUSTAINING A SUPERIOR CUSTOMER SERVICE ORGANIZATION

CREATING AND SUSTAINING A SUPERIOR CUSTOMER SERVICE ORGANIZATION

A Book about Taking Care of the People Who Take Care of the Customers

Jim Poisant

Q

QUORUM BOOKS
WESTPORT, CONNECTICUT • LONDON

Library of Congress Cataloging-in-Publication Data

Poisant, Jim.
 Creating and sustaining a superior customer service organization : a book
 about taking care of the people who take care of the customers / Jim Poisant.
  p. cm.
 Includes bibliographical references and index.
 ISBN 1–56720–450–3 (alk. paper)
 1. Customer services. 2. Organizational effectiveness. I. Title.
 HF5415.5.P63 2002
 658.8'12—dc21   2001019866

British Library Cataloguing in Publication Data is available.

Copyright © 2002 by Jim Poisant

All rights reserved. No portion of this book may be
reproduced, by any process or technique, without the
express written consent of the publisher.

Library of Congress Catalog Card Number: 2001019866
ISBN: 1–56720–450–3

First published in 2002

Quorum Books, 88 Post Road West, Westport, CT 06881
An imprint of Greenwood Publishing Group, Inc.
www.quorumbooks.com

Printed in the United States of America

The paper used in this book complies with the
Permanent Paper Standard issued by the National
Information Standards Organization (Z39.48–1984).

10 9 8 7 6 5 4 3 2 1

To
my wife and best friend Elaine
and to our wonderful family,
Juliet,
Patrick and his wife Connie,
Christopher and his wife Molly

Contents

Preface

Empires don't exist because there are great individuals who force their leadership upon resistant followers. Empires exist because individuals want to be part of a group, want to have the security that can only be had if one is part of a group, want to be held in high esteem by those above and below them in the group's pecking order, and want a place to build and lead—even if they are not the supreme builder or leader that history will remember.

Lester Thurow, *Head to Head*
(Former Dean, School of Business)

First and foremost this book is about *human beings*: their motivations, feelings, needs, spirit, loyalty, and productivity. It is also about those who *manage* human beings, their motivation, loyalty, attitudes, and behavior.

It's rare in past and present businesses and organizations to come across workers who are truly pleased with their management. It is even more rare to find someone who can tell you that they've had a long succession of great, or even good, managers throughout their careers. The negative stories and jokes about bosses are bountiful. But, it's my belief that unhappiness in the workplace and unflattering stories about managers would change if managers better understood *how* to manage and motivate their people. I feel that the current set of beliefs, values, and practices of managers, based on past beliefs and practices that have evolved over time, is incorrect.

Like countless others who have either chosen or have been thrust into the management profession, I've learned what I know about management through the day-to-day vagaries of what is usually called the "school of hard knocks"—a haphazard, sometimes rough-and-tumble approach to accumulating a coherent body of knowledge.

While I am aware that there is a certain truth in the old adage that "there's nothing like being burned by a hot stove to understand that intense heat really hurts," I question the value of so many of us in management placing our hands on the "searing hot stove," of mismanagement to learn that our actions can cause ill will, physical illness, and other negative effects on our organizations, ourselves, employees, and customers.

There are those who might argue that lessons learned that way are the most enduring. But I had long suspected the existence of a body of knowledge being used in superior customer service organizations that would negate that idea. All I had to do was figure out what those organizations were doing and why. In other words, what were their "secrets" to success?

The path to discovering those "secrets" to service excellence wasn't easy. I found partial answers in a large number of places—in history, textbooks, biographies, case studies, management theories, consulting studies, successful executives, successfully and unsuccessfully run organizations, and from a number of other graduates from the "school of hard knocks." But none offered answers that any manager—at any level, in any organization—could consistently use effectively.

Bookstores and libraries are filled with management tomes devoted to a wide variety of management topics that range from *In Search of Excellence* to *The One-Minute Manager*. However, no one book has been able to present a logical, easily understood blueprint for creating and sustaining a superior customer service organization.

It wasn't until I began working for the Walt Disney Company in Orlando, Florida, in the mid-eighties that I realized that such a book could be written. This book would serve as a blueprint for all managers at all levels for most management decisions, a work that could eliminate the long learning curve and countless errors of the "school of hard knocks."

This book closely examines the major elements of an organization and shows how they foster or hinder the organization's ability to render superior service. It also examines management from an historical perspective in the sense that such things as economic cycles, events, and the American culture have influenced the management profession. The elements under review include:

Gaining Perspective
The Role and Attitude of Management
The Organization's Mission
Corporate Culture
Customer Experiences
Employee Experiences
Organizational Structure
Communications
Staffing
Training and Orientation
Recognition and Discipline Practices
Organizational Language
Time
Reinforcing and Changing Culture

Finally, I discuss how the Information Age will impact organizations, those in management and customer service in the 21st century. Most chapters finish with a Key Points section intended as a quick reference for the reader.

I ask that the reader take the message in this book to heart and be patient. There's nothing here that hasn't been proven to work if applied with the right attitude. I've validated what I learned from Disney and other superior customer service organizations time and again over the past 15 years. More important, I've been successful in actually implementing what I've learned with outstanding results in a variety of businesses and organizations.

My goal is for this book to be used as a key reference by those in management. Although the subject matter may appear broad, the real examples I have used are quite specific and serve to underscore the central themes of managing superior customer service organizations.

I want to make it clear that I don't pretend to have all the answers. But this is a sound approach to managing successfully and a good starting point for new or seasoned managers to begin improving. For those new to management it should provide you with a giant head start. For those of you in management it will serve you well.

I'd like to thank you in advance for reading this book. I sincerely hope you enjoy it and put its teachings to use.

Acknowledgments

There are a number of people that I would like to acknowledge as being influential and supportive of this book. First and foremost, I would like to acknowledge my wife Elaine for her support, encouragement, and patience. This book has taken me countless hours to write, hours that could have been spent helping out or spending time together.

My heartfelt gratitude and endearing love to my mother Marguerite and father Henry. Your lessons of working hard, fairness, and empathy paid off in many ways.

To my in-laws Mary and Paul Quinn for their phenomenal job of instilling the highest values, standards, and integrity in their daughter.

Thanks to Dr. Andres Fortino of George Mason University's School of Management for recommending this book to Jim Dunton of Quorum Books (Greenwood Publishing Group). My sincere appreciation to Greenwood Publishing Group, for electing to publish the book. In particular, I would like to acknowledge Dr. James Sabin and Marcia Goldstein for managing and leading the publishing process. Special thanks also go to Katie Chase for her expert editing and suggestions. Katie is an outstanding editor and a great coach.

Sincere appreciation goes to Dr. Terry Domzal, the former Dean of the School of Management at George Mason University, for providing personal encouragement, editorial support, and an opportunity to be part of the faculty at the School of Management.

Over the years, I have had the opportunity to work on great teams. Each team member contributed to making dreams and visions come to life through their hard work and dedication. My sincere appreciation and gratitude go to the wonderful EDS team of more than 300 professionals who created, built and operated the EDS Information Technology Pavilion located within the Infomart building in Dallas, Texas. This outstanding team was responsible for creating and building the finest marketing center of its type in the world. Although members deserve to be individually recognized, it would not be feasible to name them all. However, I would like to mention a few. First, Bonnie Arvin, the Assistant Director of the Pavilion, for her dedication, enthusiasm, and support of the vision. Another very important person is Sandie Mayfield, who has remained a close family friend over the years. Other key members of the team include Larry Lozon, Brian Baldwin, Janet Branstetter, Darrel Thomas, Mike Willis, Andrea Hendrix, Kent Matthews, Craig Savage, Mike Carter, Jim Pullum, Sanjay Lobo, Lewis McWhite, Kelly McCann, Jeff Wacker, Todd Furniss, Rob Stewart, Tammis Lewis, Pat Williams, Lori Preston, Guy Thomas, Del Schuler, Pat Adams, and last but not least Kathy Korioth.

In addition to the EDS staff there were scores of contractors involved in the construction of the Pavilion. I would like to acknowledge one in particular, the prime design and building contractor, the Museum Arts Company of Dallas, Texas. Special thanks to the management team of Charles Paramore, Terry Brown, Terry Gilliam, and my life-long friends, Mike and Peggy Ruff. The success of the Infomart project can be summed up in the words of Stanley Marcus of Neiman Marcus fame after visiting the Pavilion. "This facility is among the finest quality I have ever seen." It is difficult at best to describe what this team accomplished. In my opinion, it was nothing less than miraculous.

Accomplishments come from challenges and opportunities. There are those who get credit for their accomplishments and there are those who provide the opportunities to begin with. In my case, I would like to acknowledge those who have given the teams and me the opportunities to succeed. To Ron Verner and John Castle, for their trust in me and their never-ending support of the EDS Pavilion team.

To Les Alberthal, the retired Chairman and CEO of EDS, for his leadership, vision, and support of the Information Technology Pavilion and for reviewing this book. To George Newstrom, Corporate Senior Vice President, EDS who originally approached me to write the proposal for the United States (Fairfax County, Virginia) to host the 1998 World Congress on Information Technology. As Chairman of this World Congress, George led the charge for the world-class legacy of the 1998 congress. To Harris Miller, President of the Information Technology Association of America and recipient of the 1998 World Congress award, for entrusting and wholeheartedly supporting the team and me in particular throughout the entire effort to prepare and produce the 1998 World Congress on Information Technology. To Pat Woolsey, the former Chairman of the Fairfax County Economic Development Authority, for her trust and support.

To Mark Grady, Dean of the School of Law at George Mason University, for his personal and professional support, guidance, encouragement, and vision. I would also like to acknowledge Dr. Alan Merten, President of George Mason University and Bradford Brown, Chairman of the National Center for Technology and Law for allowing Poisant International to have the opportunity to work on the Global Internet Summits. Others to be acknowledged from George Mason University are Helen Ackerman, Barbara Lubar, Keith Segerson, Julie Gladback, Rob Auchter, Stephen Parr, Joy Hughes, Fred Wintrich, Raymond D'Souza, Norm Barns, Behnaz Ghahramani, and Walt Galanty.

To my good friends Bob Laurence, Chairman Emeritus of the World Information Technology and Services Alliance, Al Berkeley, Vice Chairman of the Nasdaq Stock Market for their personal and professional support of the World Congresses and reviewing this book. I thank Jack Marsh, former Secretary of the United States Army, and William Marre, the cofounder of the Covey Leadership Center for their reviews as well. Thanks to William Cohen, former U.S. Secretary of Defense, for his comments related to the 2001 Global Internet Summit.

Special recognition and thanks go to Deborah Jacroux at Microsoft for all her friendship, support, and assistance in scheduling senior Microsoft executives, including Bill Gates, to participate in our events.

Sincere appreciation also goes to Tom Byrne who diligently worked to get my thoughts legible in the early draft stages of this book.

George Wackenhut, the Chairman of the Wackenhut Corporation, gave me my first opportunity as part of a large corporate management team. George not only gave me an opportunity, he provided me with an outstanding business role model.

I owe the Disney Company a great deal of thanks for allowing me to become a "cast member" and take part in perhaps the greatest example of an organization that created and sustains a superior customer service organization.

Special acknowledgment goes to the finest full-service international events management and development teams anywhere. The core members of the United States 1998 World Congress on Information Technology and the Global Internet Summit teams were Keith Bodamer and Laura Verinder. Keith is by far the most successful, and hardest working business development executive in the business. Laura's total dedication, extreme hard work, and accomplishments rank her among the best international event coordinators and administrators anywhere. I would like to mention that the tremendous results achieved by both Laura and Keith would not have been possible without the support of their spouses, Syd and Mimi. Thanks to both for all their support. Other star staff members are wholeheartedly acknowledged: Howard Sulkin, Barbara Burke, Connie Poisant, Sue Koster, Heather Glynn, Wendy Gillette, Katie and Amy Verinder, and our student interns.

Sincerest appreciation from the heart is given to the best event production anywhere to Steve Aberg, Meg Galanty, Dominique Corbin, Mac Mackenzie, Butch and Debbie Palmer, Matt Dwyer, Dorothy Reardon, and Margaret Fletcher. To Jean Haney and Jessica Johnson for their fine work on organizing and editing this book. Thanks and appreciation to Warren Martin for his friendship and continuing support from Price Waterhouse Coopers. Sincere appreciation goes to Susie, Melissa, and Gene Supernor, Diana and David Propeck, and Maury and Diane Zeitler for their never-ending encouragement and support.

I owe a great deal to Dr. Jerry Gordon, President of the Fairfax County Economic Development Authority. For years, Dr. Gordon has been a true friend and personal supporter of a number of events including the World Congress (1998) the Global Internet Summits (2000, 2002), and the Emerging Business Forum.

Leadership and management teams richly deserve recognition. In most cases they get it. However, there is another group of individuals who ordinarily do not get the appropriate recognition—they are the front-line employees. This entire book would be a contradiction, if I did not acknowledge the vital importance of the front-line staffs of organizations. It is the front-line that has the most to do with the success of most accomplishments of organizations and businesses-not management. Therefore the most special recognition and acknowledgment go to those people who take care of the customers—the front line. Extraordinary accomplishments come from ordinary people who are managed with care.

Chapter One

Gaining Proper Perspective

As we advance deeper into the knowledge economy, the basic assumptions underlying much of what is taught and practiced in the name of management are hopelessly out of date.

Peter F. Drucker
Forbes Magazine, October 5, 1998

ROOTS OF AMERICAN MANAGEMENT

Before I discuss the "secrets" of superior customer service organizations, it's important that you possess an understanding of the evolution of management attitudes and practices. In other words, what has happened in the past that has shaped the present? How did we get here? Why do managers behave the way they do? Without a comprehensive understanding of where management values, behaviors, and beliefs have come from, you cannot hope to gain the perspective necessary to change them.

Management beliefs and behaviors are deeply rooted within societal cultures. But, where did the values of cultures come from in the first place? Most managers can't answer this question. The reality is that managers do things the way they have always been done because they don't know any differently. As new organizations are formed, established values, practices, and behaviors are simply transferred. It's true that a new culture emerges in every new organization, but, unfortunately the new organizations contain variations of existing beliefs and practices. The behavioral characteristics of individuals and organizations are controlled by what I call "an invisible force field." This force field works on the assumption that activities within the organization occur just because that is *the way things are done here.*

One way to illustrate this point is through a study done about the behavior of five apes. The author chose to be anonymous. It goes something like this:

> *Start with a cage containing five apes. In the cage, hang a banana on a string and put stairs under it.*
>
> Before long, an ape will go to the stairs and start to climb toward the banana. As soon as he touches the stairs, spray all of the apes with cold water. After a while, another ape makes an attempt with the same result—all the apes are sprayed with cold water.
>
> Turn off the cold water. If, later, another ape tries to climb the stairs, the other apes will try to prevent it even though no water sprays them.
>
> Now, remove one ape from the cage and replace him with a new one. The new ape sees the banana and wants to climb the stairs. To his horror, all the other apes attack him.
>
> After another attempt and attack, he knows that if he tries to climb the stairs, he will be assaulted.
>
> Next remove another of the original apes and replace it with a new one. The newcomer goes up the stairs and is attacked. The previous newcomer takes part in the punishment with enthusiasm.
>
> Again, replace a third ape with a new one. The new one makes it for the stairs and is attacked as well. Two of the four apes that beat him have no idea why they were not permitted to climb the stairs, or why they are participating in the beat-

ing of the newest apes. After replacing the fourth and fifth original apes, which have been sprayed with cold water, no ape ever again approached the stairs. Why not? Because that's the way it's always been around here.

The fact that things have always been done a certain way does not necessarily mean that they're right, fair, or intelligent. You may be asking, "So what? What does this have to do with creating and sustaining superior customer service organizations?" The answer is quite simple. We as human beings have an instinctive need to be accepted by others—in the workplace as well as in society. We tend to act in ways we think others will approve of. Think of how young lovers behave toward each other. Think of how some managers behave in front of the chairman of the board. Think of how a new employee behaves on his or her first day. People behave in certain ways in order to be accepted by others. This fact about human nature combined with the fact that *things have always been done like this* creates corporate cultures. Cultures (values and practices) then regenerate themselves based on *the past*.

It is my strong belief that because managers have no point of reference other than existing values and practices, they have no choice but to continue within their present "force field." They are lemmings running over a cliff, following the person who preceded them.

The force field condition helps to explain why superior organizations are so rare and why they attract so much attention. They have somehow found a way to correctly create and sustain their organizations. I am convinced that these organizations were successful because management acted more on instinct, economic condition, or genius, rather than perpetuating an existing culture. So it is imperative that managers understand the past in order to understand how to change the present. Managers must be able to identify and focus on those elements of their organizations that are hindering or helping the organization.

So, what did happen in the past that influences the way managers act today? The only way to find the answer is to go back and examine our past. I, like most people, get bored easily with history if I'm just asked to memorize places and dates. So this chapter is not a history lesson. I don't pretend to be an historian. What I will do is share a personal perspective with you. I hope you'll come away with a perspective that will assist you in understanding management, as it exists today. Come with me now as we search for the roots of our management ancestry. I think that you'll be amazed as I was at how little a span of time there is to examine.

TIME IS MONEY (LATE 19TH–EARLY 20TH CENTURIES)

In the late 19th century America was being transformed from an agrarian society to an industrial society. Management as we know it today, with its command and control and hierarchical organizational structures, took shape during the Industrial Revolution that began in the late 19th century. There were a few notable exceptions, however, appearing prior to 1900.

One that comes to mind is Cyrus McCormick. McCormick invented the reaper, which revolutionized the farming industry and allowed for the U.S. Midwest to become the "breadbasket" of the world. McCormick was the first to offer free trials, warranties, and color ads. He didn't have a management manual to refer to when he had a question or a challenge. His instinct, genius, common sense, and hard work were responsible for his success.

His salesmen were his lifelines to his customers, and the quality and service of his reaper determined his success. He also knew his customers. Being a farmer himself, he knew the impact of a machine breaking down. He knew that the only way he'd be able to make his company grow was by serving his customers' needs. His entire enterprise was based on the goodwill farmers had toward the McCormick Company as a whole, not on Cyrus McCormick himself. Therefore, everyone working for McCormick represented him. He must have been a good manager. He must have been good to his employees. It wouldn't be a stretch to say that the McCormick Company was a superior customer service organization. Keep this in mind as we go through the 20th century and try to identify the next time we come across a superior customer service organization.

When the 20th century began, the United States was being led by an imperialist. President Theodore Roosevelt believed that the United States should be an empire and that war was noble. Congress proclaimed war on Spain and set about to build the Panama Canal. This sense of authority and confidence, combined with bold action, fueled the spirit of U.S. expansion. Roosevelt provided a role model for those in management. Be BOLD, confident, and take what you want, was his message. He honestly believed that the United States had the *right* to rule the world.

In 1900 there were only 11 miles of concrete highway in the United States. That changed when Henry Ford built the Model T. By 1901 the United States led the world in every industrial product, millions of Americans were at work, and the United States was the most inventive nation in the world. Many compared that time to the great Renaissance of Europe. The electric light, telephone, telegraph, and the airplane were invented in the early 1900s.

At this time, however, there was an extremely adversarial relationship between labor and management. We get a glimpse of management's attitude toward workers by reading Andrew Carnegie's credo:

> "Watch your costs and profits will take care of themselves." Translation: make the trains bigger; run them faster; cut wages; make employees work longer, 13 hour days, seven days a week. They can take July Fourth off. Carnegie inspired competition among his plant employees. If a crew fell behind, its members would be fired. He hired men to act as spies among the workers. (*Washington Post*, January 19, 1977)

During this period we saw mass production, smoke- and soot-filled skies over factories and cities, and deplorable living and working conditions for most workers. Yet it was at the turn of the century that we saw the largest migration of immigrants in American history. Some 13 million immigrants arrived on U.S. soil with nothing but the clothes they wore and what they could carry in a few suitcases. They were fleeing starvation and tyranny. Compared to today's working conditions, the conditions early in the 20th century were horrid. But to the immigrant the conditions were an improvement. Workers at the time felt fortunate simply to have jobs. Asking for health benefits, sick leave, or vacations wasn't even thought of, either by the workers or, especially, by management. In 1910,

> Frederick W. Taylor who called himself the "father of scientific management" was being hailed by industry and cursed by labor. Trained as an engineer, Taylor had increased the efficiency of many factories by close observation of individual workers with the idea of eliminating all wasted time and motion. Workers objected to having all their movements studied with a stopwatch yet companies took Taylor's ideas and implemented them. (*Chronicle*, 1989, p. 569)

In 1911 a horrible fire broke out at the Triangle Shirtwaist Company in New York City—146 women died in the blaze. Many of the victims leapt to their deaths grasping their paychecks in their fists. "The building was said to be fireproof, but there was no sprinkler system and one of the two doors was locked to keep the ladies from sneaking out with a spool of thread" (*Chronicle*, p. 570). The conditions at the turn of the century obviously did not favor the well-being of employees. There was no need to give them anything more than the bare minimum to keep them coming back to work. Management was much more interested in increasing production and profits. There was very little attention paid to workers in the early parts of the 20th century. When it was it was focused not on the employees' well-being but on how to increase production to earn more profits.

Keep a few other things in mind about this period of time. Women were not allowed to vote or own property. Women teachers were not allowed to live by themselves; if they did they would be fired. If a person was fortunate enough to be in school, it was either shop for boys or typing for girls. Blacks, other minorities, and poor whites were being discriminated against and abused. There were numerous incidents of lynching. Racism was rampant. It was a man's world, but only if you happened to be a well-off white man.

The United States entered World War I in 1917. Britain praised America's entry into the war. "Prime Minister David Lloyd George said that 'America has at one bound become a world power in a sense she never was before' " (*Chronicle*, p. 599). Over 1.4 million women worked on everything from assembly lines to delivering coal. In 1918 the Supreme Court of the United States did something unthinkable. It struck down the Keating-Owen child labor law with the judgment that Congress cannot "control the states in their exercise of the police power over local trade and manufacture." Out of nearly 2 million working children only 20 percent or so worked in mines and factories. But it was there that the conditions were the worst. Kids in Southern mills got doused with cold water when they dozed off during the night. Ten-year-old boys struggled to pick sharp slate off of speeding coal belts 14 hours a day (*Chronicle*, p. 604). In 1918 the war ended at a cost of 50,585 American lives.

As we moved into the twenties we witnessed substantial gains in U.S. productivity. This was primarily due to mechanization and an abundance of cheap labor. Wages were very low. The notable exception was the Ford Motor Company, paying its workers an unheard of wage of $5 a day. In other factories it was commonplace for people to work 6 days a week, 12–18 hours a day, for $2 a day.

In 1920 women were denied admission to the ceremony to ratify the 19th Amendment, giving them the right to vote, at the home of the secretary of state, but it passed.

Two million children, some as young as four years old, worked in factories. There were no safety precautions taken for workers. It was commonplace to see children with maimed or amputated limbs.

In the early twenties personnel specialists formed the American Management Association. It is interesting to note that personnel specialists rather than managers formed this association. Mary Parker Follett (1868–1933), respected political and social philosopher, was sought after on the business lecture tour for her advice on organizational problems.

Her approach was to analyze the nature of the *consent* on which any democratic group is based by examining the psychological factors underlying it. The consent, she suggested, is not static, but a continuing process, generating new and living group ideas through interpenetration of individual ideas. Well in advance of her time, she contended that final authority inhering in the chief executive should be replaced by an authority or function in which each individual has final authority for his own allotted task. (Heyel, 1973, p. 256)

In 1926 Ford reduced the workweek to 40 hours, five days a week. The unions praised it and some industrialist condemned it (*Chronicle*, p. 631).

In 1927 Elton Mayo conducted studies of the monotonous working conditions of factory personnel at Western Electric's Hawthorne plant in Cicero, Illinois. The studies, known as the Hawthorne Studies,

in their various phases called into serious question a number of assumptions as to the nature of the worker and his work. The studies indicated that there was revelation that the worker is no mere "economic man" motivated solely by the paycheck. A second recognition was that of the singular importance of individual attitudes in the determination of behavior. A third was the importance of the supervisor's role in the equation of morale and productivity. (Heyel, 1973, p. 380)

THE GREAT DEPRESSION TO WORLD WAR II
(1929–1940)

We saw little or no change in working conditions or civil rights. In 1929 the Stock Market crashed, giving way to the Great Depression. One can only imagine the conditions in the workplace during this time. One thing is for sure, whatever values, practices, and attitudes that management had prior to the Great Depression were reinforced during it. Stop just for a minute and think. Was there anything in the twenties that caused any behavior or institutional changes in managers or businesses? The answer is no. So, things continued to be done, *the way things have always been done*.

As we entered the thirties abuse of workers reached the boiling point. All across the country hundreds of thousand of workers struck against management. Some strikes resulted in deaths of workers and police. In response to the labor unrest the federal government passed the Wagner Act, which protected the right of workers to form unions. For most of the decade Franklin D. Roosevelt struggled with recovering from the Great Depression.

In 1938 Chester Barnard sent yet another wake-up call to American managers in his book, *Functions of the Executive*. Barnard presented an analysis of how organizations should be led. He argued against top-down management edicts in favor of eliciting cooperation from the workforce. Bernard joined Follett and Mayo in recommending that management should change the way they manage and treat their people.

GLOBAL NIGHTMARE

By the end of the decade America was on the verge of entering World War II. As far as the profession of management was concerned, everyone's energy was focused on stopping Hitler and the Japanese. In 1938 Hitler marched into Austria. It was broadcast on radio and newsreels, so few Americans were unaware of what Hitler was doing in Europe. In 1939 Germany invaded Poland, and England announced that it was at war with Germany. In 1941 the United States entered the war. In December 1940 the first peacetime draft occurred in the United States. To America and the world the future of democracy was at stake.

It's easy to understand what was occurring within America's businesses: everything and everyone had to be focused on winning the war. Millions of American men were going off to war and some 3.5 million women temporarily performed nontraditional roles working in factories. Rationing took place, yet there was a sense of nationalism in the United States. Extensive government controls were imposed during the war. However, race riots rocked New York, Los Angeles, and Detroit. "In two days in Detroit 35 people were killed and 600 were wounded" (*Chronicle*, p. 712). In another incident in Detroit, "a white protest against employment of Negroes was put down by federal troops, with another loss of 35 lives" (p. 708). Production doubled and the ENIAC (general-purpose computer) was invented in 1943. During this period the gap between rich and poor began to decline.

Perhaps the most referred to and most relevant 20th-century theory for those of us in management is Abraham H. Maslow's "A Theory of Human Motivation" (1943, pp. 370–396). Maslow observed that "man is a wanting animal" and that one desire is no sooner satisfied than another takes its place. He noted that human beings have a sense of order and a succession of motives. Human beings begin with basic needs and move up Maslow's Hierarchy of Needs:

5. **Self-Actualization Needs**: The peak of human existence; the ability to develop latent capabilities and realize one's fullest potential.
4. **Esteem Needs**: Psychological well-being, built on the perception of oneself as worthy and recognized by others.
3. **Love or Belonging Needs**: Beyond existence needs lies the desire for nurturing acceptance, respect, and caring relationships.
2. **Safety Needs**: Need to be free from harm or danger, to have a secure and predictable life.
1. **Physiological Needs**: Most basic is the need for relief from thirst, hunger, and physical drives.

All human beings have basic needs for air, water, and food. As you move up the hierarchy it's hard to argue with Maslow that human beings seek to satisfy their instinctive needs in his order.

Since first becoming familiar with Maslow's "Theory of Human Motivation," I have been continually disappointed that managers continue to either totally ignore Maslow, don't care to read him, or simply don't understand how to benefit from his work. As a student of management the message I've taken from Maslow is that people within a work environment, and in life in general, have different needs at different times. If managers want to provide motivation for employees, they need to understand where workers are within the hierarchy of needs. In other words, it would be ludicrous to attempt to motivate someone with a plaque if they can't breathe or are choking on a chicken bone. Likewise, it would be futile to expect employees to be motivated if they fear for their jobs. Instead, what managers tend to do is to give everyone the same percent raise or hand out the same plaque, even though some people deserve and *need* different forms of recognition. Furthermore, a manager's attempts to motivate may backfire, resulting in demoralizing workers. I will go into further detail on the subject of recognition in Chapter Fourteen. For now however, understand that Maslow's Hierarchy has been around for decades, yet it is generally ignored by managers.

Until the mid-forties, the values, practices, and attitudes of managers hadn't fundamentally changed since the turn of the century. The overt intensity of the adversarial relationship between management and workers subsided during the war. With the country at war it would have been perceived as unpatriotic. However, in 1946, when the nation found itself readjusting to peace, it was plagued by war at home. "Aided by tax breaks, industry enjoys healthy profits; and despite postwar layoffs, unemployment hovers below 5% percent. In 1946, 4.5 million workers struck against management crippling the coal, auto, electric, and steel industries and interrupting rail and maritime transport. Man-days lost to strikes mounted to 113 million" (*Chronicle*, p. 732).

After the war the U.S. economy boomed. Prosperity was primarily related to pent-up demands of millions of American consumers. America had also saved money during the war and was ready to spend it. The Marshall Plan for the rebuilding of Europe was unveiled in 1947. Being that U.S. factories were running efficiently enough to support the war effort, they were prepared for peacetime production. Keep in mind that the U.S. production capabilities were not attacked, unlike their Japanese and European counterparts. Therefore, in addition to supplying the voracious appetite of Americans for goods, U.S. factories were also providing products and services to rebuild other nations. Life was getting better in America (unless of course you were one of the thousands of young men heading toward the Korean War, or you were a minority). If you were a black student attending school in Gary, Indiana, in 1945 you would have witnessed about 1,000 white students protesting at Froebel School, boycotting classes in an effort to have their Negro classmates transferred to other schools. You would have also witnessed a beleaguered President Truman asking Congress for legislation to curb strikes.

Starting in the mid-forties corporations began growing nationally and internationally. That trend hasn't yet abated. In 1946 the GI Bill of Rights provided a boost to educational opportunities for the middle class. And, of course, the late forties signaled a huge Baby Boom. When the Baby Boomers reached adulthood they would do something their parents and grandparents would have never done—they questioned authority.

As we leave the forties we find labor and management relations still adversarial. In 1949, 500,000 steelworkers went on strike.

THE FIFTIES, "THE HAPPY DAYS"

Keep in mind that a number of today's senior executives in America grew up in the fifties. Chances are you as a manager are influenced each day by the values, beliefs, and practices of these individuals.

In 1950 the United States was in yet another war—in Korea. The war ended late in 1953 with the loss of over 22,000 American men. I surmise that the reason the war got so little attention from the public, with the exception of those who had to fight in it, was that the country was simply tired of war. The general U.S. population didn't want to hear about it.

In the late forties and early fifties the expectation of lifetime employment was shared both by businesses and workers. It was common to have successive generations employed by the same company. Millions of American workers began expecting that they would receive pensions as a just reward for their contributions to their companies. As corporations grew, middle managers gained more power within organizations.

In 1953 the concept of Employee Counseling was introduced to American business. So were Divisional Accounting and Profit and Loss Statements (P&Ls). For most managers today the P&Ls have become the main focus of their lives. Now you know where the bane of your existence—the infamous Profit and Loss Statement—originated. In the fifties President Eisenhower authorized the national highway system, which expanded suburbs and gave Americans the ability to take to the open highways and travel across America.

The social climate was tentative. The country had been through a hellacious war. Returning GIs wanted peace more than anything else; they wanted to raise their families in peace. The last thing they were inclined to do was to question management. Many were happy just to be alive. Like the millions of immigrants—many of the GIs' grandparents—who had come from worse circumstances, they couldn't imagine questioning their bosses. The fifties was a time for conformity. Hundreds of thousands of tract homes were built and "keeping up with the Joneses was a must." If you worked for IBM at that time you could have worn any kind of shirt you wanted to as long as it was white. Business executives were expected to have a martini or two over lunch. If you ordered a Perrier . . . well you just wouldn't.

The fifties were an unprecedented time of prosperity in America. Marketers were able to use the mass medium of television, and market research became part of doing business for ever-growing corporations. In 1955, Robert Katz in his Harvard Business School article "Skills of an Effective Administrator" argued that "training, not personality traits, makes the manager." Katz, unlike Maslow, Follett, and Mayo, veered from the notion that to effectively manage, managers needed to have a better understanding of the human needs of their employees. Instead Katz appears to be saying that everything that needs to be understood about management can be learned in training courses.

The fifties marked a number of significant events for blacks in the United States. 1952 was the first in 71 previous years that there wasn't a lynching of a black person (*Chronicle*, p. 758). In 1954 the U.S. Supreme Court struck down the long-standing "separate but equal" policy as unconstitutional, and in 1957 federal troops were sent to Little Rock, Arkansas, to help intergrate schools.

Elvis Presley was crowned the "King of Rock and Roll." Two years prior he was a truck driver making $35 a week. He was king to the young and a threat to a conformist society. "Music critics called him 'unspeakably untalented' and vulgar, a clergyman called him 'a whirling dervish of sex' " (*Chronicle*, p. 772). Rock and Roll was an important turning point in America.

Young people wanted to express themselves. They wanted their own identities, as most new generations tend to want. The youth didn't know or care much about wars or depressions; they only knew peace and prosperity. Their parents did a great job of insulating them from the harsh realities of the world, and it was their turn to break away from the conformity of their parents. Few young people in the fifties questioned authority. They just wanted to dance.

In 1957, while American youth were dancing and watching the hugely popular television show *American Bandstand*, the Russians launched *Sputnik*. The U.S. government spent an enormous amount of money to catch up. By the end of the fifties America found itself in a space race. The idea of another nation launching weapons from which the U.S. could not defend itself sent chills through those who knew the implications.

To most observers the fifties were a time of tranquility and prosperity. It was a time when America led the world. But the words a very wise, old man shared with me several years ago, "Where you stand on issues is where you sit," reminds us that all was not well in the United States. If you were a minority in the fifties there was a good chance you didn't see life through Richie Cunningham's eyes. If you were a minority in America, life in the fifties was not "Happy Days."

THE SIXTIES, "THE END OF TRANQUILITY"

The 1960s were anything but peaceful and tranquil. Everything from sex, drugs, fashion, racism, war, values, and authority—and even the president—came under serious attack. It was a time of civil unrest. College campuses erupted and cities burned. In 1960 a black civil rights worker was found hanging upside down from a tree with the letters KKK carved in his chest (*Chronicle*, p. 786). U.S. society became unraveled and an American walked on the moon.

Stop here and think. Did America's managers change their basic beliefs, values, and practices toward their workers? Hold that thought.

In 1961 a new young president was elected. In 1963 he was slain by an assassin in Dallas. In that same year Buddhist monks burned themselves alive in Vietnam in protest of the regime backed by the United States. Dozens of GIs were killed. No one could have imagined that before the U.S. involvement ended in Vietnam more than 50,000 GIs would lose their lives. In 1963 the Reverend Martin Luther King, Jr. gave his "I Have a Dream" speech to more than 200,000 listeners in Washington, DC, while Governor George Wallace stood belligerently in the doorway of the University of Alabama to block racial integration. As the decade moved on, social unrest intensified throughout the nation. The United States was "invaded" by British rock groups replacing the "King." Singer-songwriter Bob Dylan sang "The Times They Are a-Changin'."

In 1964 the Civil Rights Act was passed to combat inequities based on race, sex, color, religion, and national origin. In the meantime, racially motivated mob violence continued to erupt. Scores of people were killed and wounded.

The sixties ushered in different approaches and views on motivating employees. Theory "Y," coined by Douglas McGregor

(1959), challenged the command-and-control orthodoxies and advocated a "softer" management style—which, of course, implies that people do not need to be commanded and controlled and that managers should be nice to them.

One popular fad appearing and dying in the sixties was referred to as "sensitivity training." The idea behind this training was to bring employees together in informal gatherings, typically away from their workplace, and have them express their feelings about each other. I suppose the creators of sensitivity training courses thought that somehow people would be happier and more productive at work by being told what others thought of them. In my opinion there were several problems inherent in the method. One was that people were sometimes too honest about their true feelings and ended up hurting others, which only led to animosity back at the workplace. Another is that the focus was on the employees, *not* on those who had the most control over the motivation of the workforce—the managers. At any rate there was a lot of money spent with little to show for it. An important article appeared in the *Harvard Business Review* by Frederick Herzberg called "One More Time: How Do You Motivate Employees?" (1968). Herzberg advocated that companies could boost job satisfaction by making full use of their employees, not through sensitivity training. It sounds like Herzberg is saying the same things as Maslow, Mayo, Follett, Barnard, and McGregor: people have needs, wants, and desires. Management, in order to maximize employee contributions to the organization, must meet or exceed those needs and expectations.

As we left the sixties we found America in turmoil. President Nixon was desperately trying to get America out of Vietnam honorably, tens of thousands of American GIs had been killed or wounded, and the nation was split between the so-called silent majority (those backing Nixon) and the ever-increasing segment of the U.S. population that was against the war. The nation was at war not only in Vietnam, but, also with itself.

To some of the younger managers reading this book, it may be as difficult for you to imagine America in the sixties as it would be to imagine it in the thirties and forties. But there's a significant difference. The majority of senior managers today (your bosses) lived through the sixties in their youth. For those who experienced them, the events of the sixties impacted their values and beliefs. So it's important to keep that perspective in mind as you interact with your bosses.

THE SEVENTIES, "A TIME OF IMBALANCE"

In May of 1970 the headlines read, "Four Dead at Kent State." National guardsmen shot and killed four students on the campus of Kent State University in Ohio. In 1971, 7,000 people were arrested in Washington, DC, protesting the Vietnam War. Fifty thousand women marched on Washington demanding equal rights. Women were receiving only 58.2 percent of what men made for the same work. It was during the seventies that the Germans and Japanese emerged as formidable competitors to American business and the Consumer Movement began. Consumers sought protection through the restraint of abuses by businesses. There was growing attention by American businesses to service management. There was an ongoing shift to a service-oriented economy. That is, as competition intensified consumers were expressing discontentment about the way they were being treated. Remember that point as you read this book. *One of the basic premises of superior customer service organizations is that they understand the importance of service in a competitive environment.*

During the seventies the United States was hit with an oil embargo that led to higher prices for gas and oil. There was a steady growth of business school graduates and the consulting business boomed. Personal computers appeared along with fiber optics, and the Three Mile Island nuclear plant had a serious accident.

In 1971 the United States Supreme Court approved busing for the integration of public schools, inciting riots as far north as Boston. In 1972, President Nixon visited China while some Americans burned their flag in protest of the Vietnam War. In that same year President Nixon won reelection by a landslide and the Watergate scandal was uncovered. B52s conducted the largest aerial assault of the entire war, and in 1973 the war ended. In 1974 Nixon resigned. The seventies brought on the deregulation of industries, forcing them to be more competitive and efficient.

Women were allowed in military academies in 1975, overturning a long-standing tradition. Elvis Presley died of drug abuse at the age of 42.

The first National Women's Conference took place in 1977 and among other things women demanded more job opportunities. It's interesting to note that in 1978, 165,000 miners ended their longest strike against coal operators. As the decade came to a close, the Japanese imbalance of trade was continuing to grow. We find that the divorce rate soared to over 69 percent. Looking back to the fifties, 97 percent of all eligible males and females were married. After all the struggles of blacks for equal rights we found in 1978 that 46 percent of the schools in America remained segregated. We also saw inflation soaring and the U.S. government bailing out the Chrysler Corporation with the biggest bailout ever. U.S. Steel closed 10 plants and laid off 13,000 workers.

THE EIGHTIES, "LARGEST LOANER TO LARGEST DEBTOR" (ONLY 20 OR SO YEARS AGO)

The eighties begin in recession. Eighteen lives were lost and $100,000,000 in damage occurred in race riots in Miami and the president of the United Auto Workers Union was appointed to sit on Chrysler's board of directors. He was the first union leader ever to be elected to a board of an American company. An all-white jury cleared Klansmen of murder and Ronald Reagan won in a landslide and survived an assassination attempt. AIDS was identified by doctors in America and France. IBM's personal computer promised to revolutionize the office. The PC did in fact spread rapidly— along with Japanese factories and investments. The first woman was appointed to the Supreme Court, though "millions of women felt that 'We the people' is an empty phrase because the Equal

Rights Amendment failed to become a reality" (*Chronicle*, p. 874). The nation's prime rate was 21.5 percent in 1981.

The poverty level in the United States reached the highest level since 1967. In 1982 recession took over and industry ground to the lowest level in 34 years. EPCOT opened in Orlando, Florida, and the names of 58,000 dead Vietnam Veterans were inscribed on a black granite wall in Washington, DC. The first black mayor was elected in Chicago and President Reagan called the Soviet Union the "Evil Empire."

Tom Peters and Bob Waterman wrote the best seller *In Search of Excellence* (1982) in response to American business failures. Waterman said that "they went searching for companies that were doing it right." He indicated that they doubted they would find examples of successful companies within the United States. Peters and Waterman (especially Peters) became icons of American management. As for the premise of this book, Peters and Waterman have come to much the same conclusion that I have come to regarding American management. Peters said it this way,

I think it is probably fair to say that we lived with a bit of a house of cards. Let's go back to the end of World War II. There had been twenty years since the Depression. There were twenty years of pent-up demand. Frankly you could have made anything and the American consuming public would have bought it, starting in 1946 and that's roughly what happened. It didn't take a whole lot of genius to run a company. During this whole time period, we built all these management techniques and devices and complex structures and made the horrible mistake of associating the structures with the success, when the success frankly was a bit of an anomaly from the environment. Looked at it another way, it was nothing less than 180% shift in the way we think about managing and leading people. The models and the metaphors of the past have been the manager as a cop, referee, a devil's advocate, as a naysayer, as a pronouncer. The words that we found in the excellent companies are the manager as a cheerleader,

as a coach, as a facilitator and as a nurturer of champions. The
drumbeat that has been so sadly missing was, it all comes
from people. (Peters and Waterman film interview, n.d.)

The only thing that I would add to these comments by Peters is
simply that "it"—meaning successful management—has ALWAYS
come from people. It didn't start after World War II.

Over 1 million immigrants were caught coming into the United
States in 1983. General Motors and Toyota agreed to form a joint
venture in the United States. The Democratic Party picked a
woman for vice president in 1984. The Republicans romped to victory with Reagan and Bush. Seventy-nine banks failed in 1984,
making the most failures since 1938. By 1985 the number of home-
less people was higher than at any time since the Great Depression.

The Cold War ended and the gap widened between executives
and other employees. The eighties witnessed numerous layoffs
and the growth of contract and temporary workers. Businesses began to focus on customer service and the U.S. steel industry was in
crisis. "American firms shift output to low-wage nations, or they
import products, becoming marketers and distributors for foreign
firms" (*Chronicle*, p. 892). In response to Japanese competition,
Congress barred Japanese construction firms from public works in
1987. President Reagan also imposed high duties on Japanese electronics.

As the eighties came to a close, women occupied 40 percent of
managerial jobs. The total number of middle-class blacks in America had more than doubled between 1969 and 1984. Stockholders
revolted and businesses adopted Codes of Ethics.

The stock market tumbled by 508 points in panic on October 19,
1987, marking the worst decline in history. Major U.S. industries
and assets were being sold to foreigners.

As the decade ended there was popular sentiment within the
United States that America was losing its greatness. In addition to
the poor economy and strength of foreign competition, crack and
other drugs plagued American cities. The income gap was widening, teen suicides were rising, the cost of living was going up, and

AIDS was killing thousands of Americans. Yet 56 percent of a Gallup poll showed that Americans accepted the situation as "the way things are going" (*Chronicle*, p. 188).

THE ROARING NINETIES (JUST YESTERDAY)

Few could imagine in the eighties that within one decade the United States would regain global economic dominance. Who would have predicted a projected budget surplus and the lowest unemployment rate in the U.S. history? Fueled by the Information Technology industry, the U.S. economy had become the envy of the world, including Germany, and especially Japan. The stock market was bullish for most of the decade. Supply-chain management appeared out of necessity to deliver supplies, products, and services to businesses and buyers quickly. The "knowledge" worker was introduced to the vocabulary of organizations. Knowledge workers are those who are able to keep up with technological advances.

The nineties brought on the need for those in management to be truly international. Businesses and industries were "globalized," in that the Internet allowed new businesses to enter markets without necessarily having physical assets. I will go into more detail regarding the implications of the Information Age on businesses and management in Chapter Sixteen. For now, however, it is important to recognize that work traditionally performed in industrial-based economics is not the same in the Information Economy.

Success in the digital economy will depend on having employees who are loyal, dedicated, and trusted. They will have to be treated with respect, dignity, and a piece of the economic pie. Organizations will require those in management to understand how to motivate their workers. I can guarantee that those who better understand how to manage people will be the most successful. I can also guarantee that many of the policies, practices, values, and beliefs regarding how to manage that existed in the 19th and 20th centuries will not cut it in the 21st century.

One important point to remember is that other countries, particularly the developing ones, find themselves facing similar conditions as the United States faced in its evolution. There are no child labor laws or protection of workers from tyrannical management practices. Working conditions are bleak and racism is rampant. You and I cannot predict their future, but having a perspective of the how the United States evolved may assist you in aiding their progress. Let me be clear in saying that I'd be the last person to say that the United States has "arrived" with respect to managing people. We have a long way to go.

I ask that you reflect on U.S. history over the past 100-plus years and ask yourself some questions. What values, practices, and beliefs about managing people took root in the United States and how have they changed/evolved over time? Did some of these values, beliefs, and practices get passed down to those who manage today? In my opinion there's no way that they could not have. I'm not saying that attitudes and practices continue to be as severe as they were in the past. But I am saying that they still exist in some form and they are to be factored into the study of management today. So, as you move forward in this book I ask that you consider the heritage of American management. I believe having this perspective will aid you greatly in understanding the force field within the "cage" in which you may have found yourself trapped throughout your career. And I hope the principles in this book will help you in breaking through the force field and out of the cage.

Chapter Two

Discovering the "Secrets" of the Magic Kingdom

What are most management seminars but show biz?
Realizing this, the Walt Disney Co. is getting into the
seminar business.

Forbes, 70th Anniversary Issue

THE DISNEY INFLUENCE

As have so many other vacationers, I traveled with my family to
Walt Disney World in Orlando, Florida, several times during the
seventies and eighties. We always had a great time and often
started planning our next trip back before we headed home. Our
favorite place to stay was Fort Wilderness, located on the Disney
property. We parked our small trailer or pitched a tent and set off to
enjoy the immaculately kept camping area.

While visiting the resort, I couldn't help but marvel at the
wonders of Walt Disney World's management. The cleanliness,
efficiency, and quality of the entire property were exceptional.
But what really caught my attention was how genuinely friendly
and helpful all the employees were. No matter where we went
or what we needed, the Disney people went out of their way to
be friendly.

On a number of occasions, while my family enjoyed the park, I spent a good deal of my time asking the employees questions about working for Disney. I wanted to know what they liked most about their jobs, how much training they had received, how they were managed, and why they seemed so happy. The entire organization fascinated me because it was the first company I had seen that appeared to be operating with a total focus on exceeding its customers' expectations.

BECOMING A MEMBER OF THE CAST

I became somewhat obsessed with finding out how Disney achieved such extraordinary quality service. My curiosity stemmed from the fact that I had managed enough people, attended enough management classes, and read enough management books to know that there were a number of things I didn't understand when it came to achieving the results that Disney had clearly established as a standard.

Over time one thing became clear to me: other than doing my own unscientific research to learn the Disney management "secrets," the only way I could possibly gain this knowledge was to become a member of the Disney organization. Unfortunately, I had no experience in the entertainment industry and the company received approximately 50,000 unsolicited resumés a year for management positions—a pool from which they hired less that 150 people, predominantly technical types.

Faced with these obstacles, I decided to pursue an indirect approach. In the late 1980s, Disney purchased the Arvida Corporation, a large land developer, headquartered in Miami where we lived. I began contacting a few people who worked for Arvida and was eventually led to a former Disney manager who had transferred to the company. He thought I would be ideal for a position opening up in the Business Seminar Division at Walt Disney World in Orlando. Up to that point, the Disney Seminars Division had primarily concentrated on children and educator audiences, but it was about to expand into business seminars. To make the move, they were looking for someone with academic credentials and a non-Disney business background who was capable of objectively comparing and analyzing the differences between the way Disney managed people and the approaches used by other companies.

Fortunately, my academic credentials as a teacher and administrator were balanced by extensive training and sales experience in the private sector. After several rounds of interviews and a detailed proposal outlining how I thought the business seminars program should be established and managed, I finally became a Disney employee—or, as all staff members are known within the company, a "cast member."

MY FIRST DISNEY SEMINAR

As part of my new job, I promptly began a two-year quest to discover the "secrets" to what had caught my attention while vacationing in Fort Wilderness. My mission at Disney was to learn how the organization was designed, created, and sustained as a superior customer service organization. The first seminar that I was responsible for was "The Disney Approach to People Management."

In fulfilling my mission, I was taught not only a great deal about the management style of the Disney organization, but also about the positive and negative dynamics of several hundred other organizations. Because I had to present Disney business seminars to external management audiences from around the world, each session provided me with invaluable feedback on what current management practices were in a wide array of organizations. Despite the wealth of information I received, one of the most powerful insights into Disney's success came one hour prior to my first seminar.

THE AUDIOVISUAL KID

Although new to Disney, I felt that my job title afforded me a certain amount of status. I had been selected out of thousands of possible applicants to manage their Business Seminar Division and speak to the "outside world" about how Disney managed its people and maintained its quality. They provided me temporary lodging at a beach house on Bay Lake, just up the block from the president of Disney World. In my mind, I had arrived and I was in charge.

On the morning of my first business seminar, everything seemed to be going great. Sixty executives representing some of the largest corporations around the world had paid several hundred dollars to hear how Disney managed its people. I was a little nervous, but confident that the seminars would be a great success. I felt I was off to a terrific start. But when I entered the seminar room I was stunned to see that it wasn't even close to being ready for the program to begin. The seminar was scheduled to start in 30 minutes and none of the audiovisual equipment—projectors, microphones, screen—was set up. Chairs were scattered about and there was only one very young man putting everything together. As the manager of the division, I felt it was my duty to "manage" the situation into shape as quickly as possible. Being that all Disney cast members wear first-name badges, it was easy to introduce myself to the young man.

The type that fits the Disney mold perfectly, Todd couldn't have been more than 20 years old. Blessed with a great smile and a friendly manner, he shook my hand, said "hello," and immediately went back to what he was doing. This was his first mistake. I expected him to stand up straight, listen intently to my every word, and agree with whatever I told him. Instead, he walked away and ignored me. Standing alone in the middle of a large room feeling insulted, ignored, and, most of all, powerless, I quickly decided that Todd and I were going to get one thing straight: I was in charge and he had better show me more respect. As I approached him and asked who his supervisor was (I didn't know what else to say), he turned around with an impatient look on his face and asked me what I did. I didn't waste any time in telling him that I was the Manager of the Business Seminar Division. But before I could continue he cut me off. "I didn't ask you what your title was," he snapped. "I asked what you did!"

I was speechless. Before coming to Disney, no subordinate, let alone a 20-year-old one, had ever questioned me. Then Todd said,

"You're new here aren't you?" I said yes. "I thought so," he responded with a slightly sarcastic tone, "Well *Jim*, I don't really have the time to train you now, but if we are going to work together I might as well clear a few things up. Sit down." Not knowing what to do, I sat down. Todd stood over me and begun what I now refer to as the beginning of my "deprogramming from American management."

CUSTOMERS DON'T CARE ABOUT YOUR TITLE

Todd started out very calmly. "Jim, pay attention. At eight o'clock, 60 executives are going to come through that door as our guests. Now, how many of our guests care what your title is?" he asked.

"None," I said.

"Well, then it seems to me that what is important is that we are ready for them to have a very productive seminar." He continued, "Would you agree?" I agreed. "Then what are you doing wasting my time with this nonsense about your title and my supervisor. Give me a hand setting up!" It was a command rather than a request, and, despite all of my views about who was in charge, I found myself popping up and following his directions without hesitation.

But Todd wasn't done. "From now on, if you plan on staying with Disney that is, when you see something has to be done, jump in and help. Then once the event or activity is over, work to improve the process for the next time. *Do you understand, Jim?*"

He was just short of yelling by the time he got to the last part, but I understood all right. The only thing I didn't know was whether to salute or fire him. But, I instinctively grasped that Todd had taught me a profound lesson in management, one that changed my behavior from that point on. He was absolutely right. It isn't titles or beach houses or corner offices that make the difference in the long run, it's *serving the customer*. And in order to provide excellent service in a way that provides a competitive advantage, the entire organization must be structured around the concept of not only satisfying but also exceeding customer expectations—right down to the 20-year-old audiovisual guy.

SUPERIOR SERVICE NOT UNIQUE TO DISNEY

That was just the beginning of what I learned at Disney, and as you read this book you'll find I have strong ties to the management style and principles I observed while working there. But if I concentrated only on Disney you wouldn't receive a full understanding of what is necessary for you to create and sustain your own superior customer service organization. After all, unlike Disney, most organizations don't sell happiness as a product.

There are many other companies and organizations providing excellent customer service, many of which I have visited and presented to. A number are used as examples throughout the book. What you will discover is that in each excellent organization there is a deliberate attempt to create and sustain positive experiences for the employees by caring about them as people and providing them with resources and encouragement to achieve the organization's goals. In turn, they will respond by providing a positive experience for the customers, one that builds loyalty and increases profits. It's not as easy as it sounds, because a lot of things need to change within an organization in order for it to work. But it can be done. This book will show you how.

Chapter Three

Mission Critical

If you don't know where you are going you will end up somewhere else.

Yogi Berra
Ted Goodman, *Forbes Book of Business Quotations*

MISSIONS DRIVE ORGANIZATIONS

Missions drive organizations. Yet most mission statements are either written for the wrong audience or aren't carried out by the organization's leadership. Most managers underestimate the power of missions. It seems a simple precept, but consider the parallels: soldiers are willing to give up their lives for the mission to protect their countries; small countries have conquered much more powerful foes when they have more compelling missions. A case in point is the Vietnam War. In the minds of the North Vietnamese soldiers, their mission was simple: the survival of their people. In the case of the United States, its mission continually changed and subsequently eroded the motivation of its soldiers and citizens. As the Vietnam War dragged on, fewer and fewer American soldiers were willing to risk their lives for an unclear mission.

NASA engineers put a man on the moon against nearly impossible odds because they had a clear mission, a deadline, and the necessary resources.

In Chapter Five, I stress the vitally important role that corporate culture plays in any organization. *At the center of the culture is its mission statement.* Missions provide us a critical piece of the puzzle in discovering the elements of *superior customer service organizations.*

> The quest to make GE the most exciting and successful enterprise on earth in this decade will be won on the factory floor, in the office, in the field, face to face with customers, with everyone understanding and focused on the essential mission of the corporation: serving customers.
>
> Janet Lowe, *Jack Welch Speaks*

MISSION STATEMENTS AND THEIR AUDIENCES

As with corporate cultures, most managers do not understand how to capitalize on their missions. Most managers do not even know what their mission statements are. Do you know what yours is?

If you as a manager can't answer this question, how do you expect employees to be able to? Unfortunately, many mission statements are written for shareholders, financial analysts, and Shakespearean scholars rather than for employees. While you need to provide your customers and investors with a description of your vision for the organization, your customers and investors do not run your organization. Mission statements must be written for those who are most affected by them: the employees who either come in direct contact with the customer or support those who do.

While conducting a Disney business seminar for 60 senior executives from a variety of businesses and industries, I asked how many knew their mission statements. One woman was very anxious to be recognized. As she stood up, she waved her organization's mission statement in the air. She told the audience that her statement had taken numerous meetings with several top executives over a year to produce. The lady was a vice president of a large Midwestern hospital. She excitedly read her hospital's mission. "The mission of our hospital is to provide the finest medical care at the most cost-effective prices." I immediately seized the opportunity to ask the audience if they or a member of their family were seriously ill, would they go to this hospital? Guess what? Not one person said they would, much to the dismay of the VP. Why? When you or a loved one is ill, you do not want to be treated by a staff of people who have cost-effectiveness as part of their mission.

A few months after the seminar, I received a call from the lady. She thanked me for pointing out the problem with her mission statement. She also told me that when she returned home she convinced the hospital executives that the statement gave the wrong message to employees and patients. The net result went something like this: "The mission of our hospital is to provide the finest health care possible within a three-state region." I think you would agree that this is a hospital where you would send a loved one.

Of course it isn't enough to just *say* that your mission is to be the finest health care provider or to produce the best widget. The real test is to create and sustain an organization that lives and breathes the mission each minute of the day.

WRITING AND MODELING AN EFFECTIVE MISSION STATEMENT

Much has been written regarding the writing of mission statements. No matter what you decide to write, two things must hold true. The *first* is that everyone in the organization must understand the mission. The *second* is that everyone, especially the management, must reinforce the mission through his or her actions. In other words, a mission cannot be effective unless everyone in the organization knows and practices it.

One thing that struck me from the first day at Disney was the focus that management put on the mission of the organization, which was "to provide the finest in family entertainment." Period. It wasn't plastered all over the place. In fact, I can't recall ever actually seeing the Disney mission ever posted outside the initial orientation training class. Instead, the Disney mission was acted out each day by the management and the cast. I observed that each management and staff decision within the organization, from hiring to maintenance, was based on the mission. A translation of the mission statement was, "It's Disney or it's not Disney" (it's the finest or it's not the finest). The cast at Disney was so committed to producing the finest possible product—whether an attraction, an entertainment act, the look of a brochure cover, or guest service—that the word "finest" became synonymous with Disney.

Many mission statements mention or allude to money. They contain statements such as "our mission is to return a fair profit to our shareholders." Leave shareholders and money making out of your mission. After all, if you are in business you obviously are in it to make money. Why even mention it? The real drawback to having money mentioned in your mission is that it is a demotivator to your front line. Think about it; unless you are willing to share your profits with your employees, leave it out of your mission. Even if you do share your profits, money is known to have a limited effect on sustaining employee motivation. It's essential that your mission motivate your employees. Establish a mission that allows your workforce to be proud of what they're doing.

IMPLEMENTING THE MISSION

If you are endeavoring to change your organization's mission and culture, then once your mission is agreed on you can begin to advertise it internally. I highly recommend you take a hard look at the culture (traditions, values, practices, attitudes) of your organization to see whether it is capable of and willing to allow your mission to be implemented. Do you have the right kind of people in management and supervisory positions willing to model the behavior necessary to convey it? If the answer is "no," I sincerely believe that creating and sustaining a superior customer service organization is a pipe dream. You must gain a consensus from everyone in management to support the mission. Management must also convey the seriousness of its commitment. It's imperative that every word spoken and every action taken measures up to your mission.

One final comment on missions: if you and your organization are serious about achieving superior results through your employees, you must be willing to *take whatever action is necessary to rid the organization of managers who intimidate or mistreat employees*. This action might well be the biggest challenge you have. This will test how committed you are to achieving excellence.

KEY POINTS

1. Write your mission statement in simple language.
2. Everyone in your organization must understand it.
3. Write your mission statement to motivate your employees, not shareholders.
4. Do not mention money in your mission statement.
5. Post your mission statement in conspicuous places. You may want to have everyone sign a sheet of paper stating they have read the mission periodically so that they will be continually reminded of its importance.
6. Management must reinforce the mission statement through their actions.
7. Do not tolerate anyone in a position of authority within the organization who mistreats employees.
8. Celebrate and reward those who live the mission.

Chapter Four

The Role of Management

We want a company that focuses on nothing but serving customers, a company where everyone feels the
thrill of winning and shares in its rewards—in the soul
as well as the pocketbook. We've got to take out the boss
element. We're going to win on our ideas not by whips
and chains.

Jack Welch
Janet Lowe, *Jack Welch Speaks*

PROVIDING A POSITIVE WORK ENVIRONMENT

This chapter will be the briefest in the book. Your role as a manger is
not complex. Contrary to popular belief, the role of management is
quite simple. Business textbooks define management's prime responsibilities as strategic planning, marketing, accounting, return
on investment, and the like. I believe, however, that providing a
positive caring working environment for employees is the single
most important role of a manager. Everything else a manager does
becomes irrelevant if the employees aren't outperforming competitors. If this doesn't occur there won't be money to account for,
products to market, or strategic plans to make.

A CARING ATTITUDE

Employees need to be the center of management's concern and attention. Sustained profit and growth is primarily stimulated by customer loyalty. Loyalty is a direct result of customer satisfaction, and the level of service provided to customers largely influences their satisfaction. In turn, motivated and productive employees create a high degree of quality service that drives customer loyalty.

Many in management have not accepted that focusing on employee motivation is the *most critical* aspect of organizational success. But when all is said and done, it is the employees who ultimately determine the success or failure of any organization. If there's one single difference between superior customer service organizations and those that are not, it's the attitude senior managers have about people. Superior leaders truly care about people. In turn, they provide a caring work environment for them.

A caring working environment is one in which employees can act without fear of being criticized or intimidated, a place where they feel free to express their opinions, make suggestions, and feel that they are counted on and respected. On the surface, this recipe for success appears to be very simple, but countless managers and scholars have struggled with how to implement the ideal balance. Organizations that focus on creating and sustaining positive employee experiences within a caring environment are solidly positioned to compete.

MANAGERS WORK FOR EMPLOYEES

Whenever I hire someone, I ask him or her to come into my office before they start work. My first question is, whom do they work for? Naturally, I get a lot of strange looks, but the inevitable answer is, You. I tell them that they are partially correct. Then I mention that my main job is to work for them. I go on to explain that my job is to encourage and train them, provide them with the resources and tools they'll need to do their jobs, and create an environment where they can be successful. I also tell them that I hate the word "boss" and then ask that they never refer to me that way, even in an introduction. It never fails to amaze me how delighted employees are afterward.

SETTING GUIDELINES FOR EMPLOYEES

Excellent managers are known for allowing their employees to be creative and empowered; however in my opinion people need guidelines that govern some behaviors. I have found it helpful to establish certain behavioral ground rules. Here are a few of mine:

Rule #1. No gossip!

Rule #2. Health comes first, family second, and work third.

Rule #3. Do not take credit for work done by others.

Rule #4. Focus on quality.

Rule #5. Exceed customer expectations.

I am fond of a saying that a wise old man once told me: "no one ever remembers how long something took to make, they will remember, however, how good it was." I have found this to be very, very good advice.

THE MANAGER BENEFITS

If you as the manager provide a caring environment for your employees from day one, it is you who will benefit the most. Typical "people problems"—high turnover, low morale, errors—which are usually caused by employees not feeling a sense of ownership in the organization and not having an overall sense of pride and commitment, are minimized. This of course benefits you. Ultimately, production increases, more money is made for the company, and you reap the benefit. This makes common sense.

Jack Welch of General Electric is referenced occasionally in this book. He is thought of around the world as the best manager in America, maybe anywhere. Welch gives the following insight to GE managers:

While facing economic realities, GE managers still must care
about the people who work for them. If they don't go out and
care about their people, the people won't do things for them.
You have to constantly show you care. The only thing that
makes our company work is the fact that our people are in the
game. We (managers) don't do it. (Lowe, 1998, p. 51)

KEY POINTS

1. Management's most important job is to provide a positive working environment for their employees.

2. Managers must sincerely care for and appreciate those with
   whom they work.

3. Excellent managers perceive themselves as working for their
   employees versus having the employees work for them.

4. Managers need to set basic behavior guidelines for their
   workforce.

5. Managers and their organizations are the true beneficiaries of
   caring work environments.

Chapter Five

Why Organizational Structures Matter

The corporation as we know it, which is now 120 years old, is unlikely to survive the next 25 years. Legally and financially yes, but not structurally and economically.
                              Peter Drucker, "Sage Advice"

TOP-DOWN MANAGEMENT

The majority of American organizations are structured in a top-down hierarchical structure. In other words, the higher one rises in this type of organization, the more authority and control one has. American workers, along with most other workers around the world, have learned to accept this hierarchical structure without question.

Some organizations lend themselves more naturally than others to hierarchical management structures. The military is a prime example, with the highest ranking person giving orders to the next highest ranking and so on down the line. This management structure makes common sense in the military. However, *it makes no sense in an organization that hopes to achieve superior customer service.*

A TRAGIC MISTAKE

Examine the structure in Figure 1 from the top down and ask yourself the following questions: Is this the best type of organization to motivate employees? Is it the best type of organization to focus on the customer? The answer to both questions is *no* because of two significant omissions.

The first is the most obvious: the customer is missing. Historically, American hierarchical organizations neglect to include the customer. The main focus is on increasing profits. In part, this legacy is a by-product of the country's historic development. American industry had little competition until the latter part of the 20th century.

Figure 1
Traditional Hierarchical Organization Structure

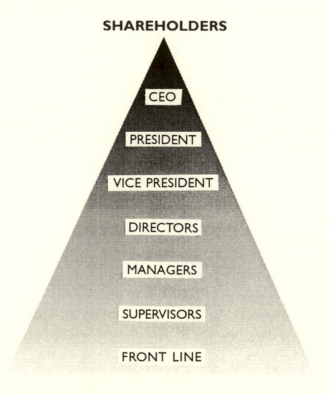

SHAREHOLDERS

CEO

PRESIDENT

VICE PRESIDENT

DIRECTORS

MANAGERS

SUPERVISORS

FRONT LINE

As Thomas J. Peters, noted for his enormously popular book, *In Search of Excellence* (coauthor Robert H. Waterman, Jr.), said in an interview, "After World War II you could have made anything and the American public would have bought it." The reason being that the war had left most of the world in a state of devastation and the domestic and international demand for American goods and services was exceptionally strong. He went on to say that American managers made the tragic mistake of equating their style of management after World War II to their success, when in fact their success was based on consumer demand. This false assumption once again reinforced the hierarchical organization structure.

The second point is that employees, like customers, were also taken for granted by American companies, evidenced by their occupation at the lowest position on the chart. Despite its reputation as a highly mobile population, post–World War II America was a land of small towns and midsized cities where people rarely migrated from their homes until well into the middle of the 20th century. Returning veterans wanted little more than a job and a modest, safe place to live and raise a family. Most any conditions veterans found in the workplace were better than those they had experienced in war.

Although the sixties brought a shift in cultural values and an increased level of mobility, it was not uncommon for workers to stay with a company for 30 years, receive their gold watch, and retire. Quite often, sons followed their fathers' footsteps and worked for the same company. The promise of long-term security was enough to provide a steady supply of employees for most organizations. This sense of worker abundance did little to call the hierarchical management structure into question.

Unfortunately, the hierarchical organizational structure fails to acknowledge the critical role that front-line employees play within the organization. The fact that front-line employees are located at the bottom of the organization insinuates that they are the least important. This fact is pretty easy to validate in your organization. Simply ask your employees who runs the organization. There is an excellent chance that the answer is *not* "they do."

One of the central liabilities of top-down management is that it places managers in the position where they are encouraged to believe that they are somehow superior to those who work beneath them. Many feel that they have all the answers regardless if they are right or wrong. This is particularly apparent when young, inexperienced managers take control. In many cases, due to insecurity, they assert their authority to make sure that everyone knows that they are in charge. In excellent organizations these incidents do not occur with much frequency because their cultures discourage this type of behavior.

During my customer service presentations I often asked audiences to focus on the hierarchical chart and tell me to describe how they would feel about themselves if they occupied each level on the chart. I began with the front line.

Inevitably, the response was negative. I then asked if there was a feeling of great pride, empowerment, and ownership of the organization among front-line staff within their organizations. The answer was always a resounding NO! In many cases there was nervous laughter, because many thought it was a joke to infer that the front line had anything at all to do with running the organization. It was generally agreed among those who held management positions that when they were on the front line they worked very hard to move up in the organization to get away from being the least thought of in their organizations.

On the other hand, as I moved up the organization chart the feelings shifted from low self-esteem to pride and a greater sense of importance. Keep in mind that throughout these discussions the customer was never mentioned. Rather, the conversation centered on who had the most authority and the highest title.

I often asked audiences to suggest how they would redesign the chart to deliver better customer service and to motivate the employees. A large number suggested that the chart should be turned upside down. In other words, let the front line run the organization. I asked the audience how practical it would be to have the front line make decisions affecting marketing, financial reporting strategic planning, and running shareholders' meetings?

FUNCTIONS OF MANAGEMENT

Common sense demands that organizations must have individuals who can make overall policy decisions. The issue is not whether there should be a hierarchical management structure in place for certain functions; the issue is *how any structure supports the employees in order to serve their customers*. In superior customer service organizations, senior management retain policy responsibilities. However, they are also responsible for reinforcing the culture and mission of the organization. I believe that the greatest sense of pride and accomplishment that a manager can have is creating and sustaining an environment for employees that motivates them to serve customers. In doing so, they create an atmosphere that is most conducive to the delivery of superior customer service, one that has an edge in today's competitive markets.

FOCUS ON THE CUSTOMER

Figure 2 depicts the organizational structure that exists within superior customer service organizations. It stands apart from the hierarchical structure for two main reasons. It puts the main emphasis where it is supposed to be—around the CUSTOMER—and it shows that the front line has the greatest effect on the customer's experience.

The first thing you'll notice is that the center of attention is the customer. The *second is the location of the front-line employees*. Instead of having the front line on the bottom of the organization, they are located close to the customer. It is here where customer service most often takes place. Front-line employees "touch" the customer continually, which results in customer satisfaction or dissatisfaction. Remember, in a competitive environment the difference between winning and losing is service. Managers typically do not render service.

The two organizational structures I have outlined have tremendous implications for managers and organizations. The pyramid, by its very nature, implies that the higher you go the more power you are granted. But power to do what? In fact, the further up you

Figure 2
Superior Customer Service Organization

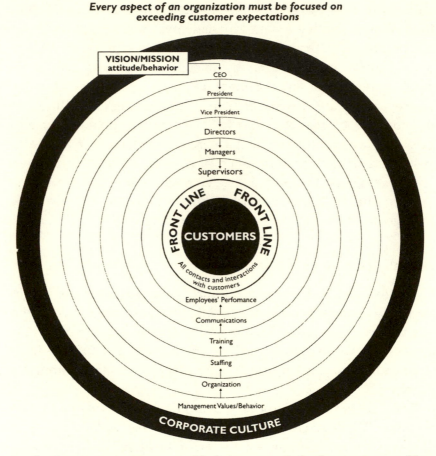

Every aspect of an organization must be focused on exceeding customer expectations

go the less power you actually have to satisfy the customer. You are totally dependant on the front line and all those who support it.

On the other hand, the circular chart implies that managers need to concentrate on how the organization services the customer through the front line. One realizes quickly that in a competitive environment the front line is truly the best weapon against competition. Successful managers must do whatever they can to control the environment (motivation) of the front line. By doing so they are in effect controlling the experience of the customer.

FRONT-LINE SUPPORT STAFF

This point was regularly demonstrated during tours of the tunnel located underneath the Magic Kingdom at Disney World in Orlando that were part of the "Disney Approach to People Management" seminars.

Beneath the park there is a large system of tunnels used primarily to move supplies and people into the different areas of the park. These tunnels allowed costumed characters to appear in the locations where they belonged without the guests seeing them walking or riding through themed areas where they would be out of place. This was just another part of the company's approach to controlling the customer's experiences and perceptions, by eliminating things that don't belong or are out of place. During the seminar tours, I pointed out the impact of the support staff on the experience of the guests by explaining that even though the people who work in the tunnels have nothing to do with the guests directly, they did have a direct impact on how the guests were treated by employees who did come in contact with the guests.

Although the delivery of supplies—food, beverages, and equipment—was central to the role of the tunnels, they also allowed costume departments to be deployed throughout the park. Every day, these departments provided all the "cast members" with fresh costumes and warm greetings and, by doing so, they were part of the circle closest to the front line. What is revealing is that Disney understands that every one in the organization has an influence on each other and that directly impacts the way the customers are treated. By embedding this appreciation into the corporate culture, the organization reinforces a commitment to superior customer service by everyone in the organization regardless if they are on the front line or six layers removed.

Do organizational structures make a difference? Sure they do. It is your choice. You can choose one that promotes support and respect for the front line or one that feeds the egos of the management.

KEY POINTS

1. Hierarchical management structures place emphasis on authority and power of the supervisory and management personnel
   with little or no regard for the front-line personnel and customers.

2. Customers are the center of attention of superior customer service organizations. Therefore, organizations must be structured
   to offer resources, support and encouragement to all employees
   in order to exceed their customers' expectations.

3. The primary responsibility of management is to reinforce the
   values and mission of the organization. Caring, supportive
   leaders best perform this function.

4. The front line is responsible for rendering customer service,
   building products, servicing products, and such. They are the
   difference between winning and losing in a competitive environment because they control the experience of the customers.

5. Organizational structures do make a difference. The way an organization is structured dictates the behavior of the employees
   and the impressions of the customers.

Chapter Six

The Heart and Soul of the Organization

Culture is simply how one lives and is connected to history by habit.

LeRoi Jones, "The Legend of Malcolm X"

CORPORATE CULTURE

Corporate culture is to an organization what an anthem is to a country: It represents the spirit, traditions, and soul of an organization. It is the foundation on which organizations are built and perpetuated. It is the most important characteristic of a company because it regulates internal behavior and governs outside impressions. It is also the most difficult element of an organization to change.

During my Disney seminar days, the subject of corporate culture was the one I most enjoyed presenting to outside audiences. I often began the sessions by providing the audience with a definition of corporate culture. "Corporate culture is defined as a common group of ideas, customs, and values shared by *all* members of a group." I would challenge the audience to describe the Disney culture by using one or two words. They consistently responded with words like "cleanliness," "pride," and occasionally "long lines" and "high prices."

WALT DISNEY'S LEGACY ADVICE

I would then invite the audience to listen to an audiotape and watch a few film clips, which contained some glimpses of Walt Disney in action. This presentation subtly revealed his nature. By understanding the man, the audience could better understand the Disney corporate culture. The audiotape was taken from "The Disney Story," one of the minor Disney World attractions located within a theater on Main St. USA at the Orlando theme park. The story is a depiction of Walt's personal and professional life in which an incident involving a young boy (Walt) who volunteered to play the trombone in a circus parade (even though he had never played the trombone before) plays a central theme. As he began to play, it was obvious he couldn't carry a tune. Needless to say, he made quite a disruptive debut.

When the band leader asked why he would do such a thing he Walt responded, "How did I know, I never tried it before." From a young age, Walt exhibited a strong tendency to take risks. Throughout his life he would take many, many more—a trait that became embedded in the culture of the company he would later found.

I also showed a film clip of an NBC interview of Walt Disney in 1966. The interviewer asked Walt what he had done to ensure the success of Disneyland after he left the organization. He responded by saying he believed his management staff was finally convinced that his management style was correct, that he believed the organization should give the guests everything it could give them, that the place should be kept immaculately clean, and that it should be a fun place to work and visit. The cultural aspects of outstanding guest service, cleanliness, and fun became the cornerstones of the Disney organization.

QUALITY EQUALS PRIDE

I also used another film clip to highlight the unique qualities of Disney's culture. The clip was of an interview with Dick Nunis, the then president of Disney World and a long-time friend of Walt's. Like the founder, Nunis stressed the importance of quality and pride as essential elements to the organization's success. He said that it was management's responsibility to provide the cast with all the support they needed to do their jobs. If management did its job properly, the cast would be able to produce quality products and services that, in turn, would instill great pride in the work force. Nunis equated the words *quality* and *pride*, believing that without one you can't have the other.

The point in sharing these vignettes was to show that a corporate culture must not only be defined by the leadership of an organization, but, it must also be believed, practiced, and continually reinforced by management at all levels. What many fail to realize is that once a corporate culture is well-defined, management's commitment to the culture becomes paramount. If part of the culture requires total dedication to cleanliness, then everyone—including those in top management positions—must pick up trash.

A HUMAN TRAGEDY IN CHICAGO

In 1989 I traveled to Chicago to address approximately 1,000 mid- to upper-level managers of a national retailer on the subject of customer service. The man who invited me was a senior vice president who had previously heard one of my presentations, and he scheduled me to speak to 500 managers in the morning and 500 in the afternoon. Before the participants entered the auditorium, each was offered coffee and pastries to bring into the session. As was customary, during my presentations I would mention that at Disney everyone would pick up papers, including managers, and that managers didn't think it was below them to help keep the place clean. Like most audiences, this one generally agreed with the concept. Yet at the end of the first speech hundreds of people walked out leaving their garbage at their places. I wasn't surprised. I found that most people agree in theory, but not always in practice.

As I exited the auditorium, I noticed a custodian entering through one of the side doors with a broom and trashcan. I immediately began helping him pick up the mess, much to the dismay of the senior vice president. I turned around and found the VP pitching in. He was embarrassed to see his guest picking up trash, and felt obliged to help. Soon there were several other executives cleaning up. As the group of helpers grew, I happened to notice the janitor. He was visibly nervous over how his newfound "helpers" got recruited. I'm sure he thought he would get in some kind of trouble having the top brass embarrassed into helping him.

Needless to say, after I mentioned the incident to the afternoon group the auditorium was left without a trace of trash. The moral of the story is simple: If Leaders agree that they should do whatever it takes to help keep the organization clean—or friendly or helpful—then they must set the example.

When I left the building the custodian met me out on the sidewalk to tell me how much he appreciated the help. With tears in his eyes, he said it was the nicest thing that anyone had done for him in the 24 years he worked for the company.

But the real point here is not that a manager went through the motions of picking up papers. Rather, it is the underlying attitude that causes the executive not to want or feel responsible to help a fellow employee. And no matter how grand the mission statement or how much money is spent on advertising, a corporate culture is nothing more than what the employees think it is—and that belief drives the type of experience that the customers receive.

A SIMPLE WAY TO KNOW YOUR CULTURE

This isn't radical news. In fact, most major U.S. corporations have realized, at least in theory, how important a well-defined corporate culture is to their organization. In the eighties in particular, there were a slew of books, articles, and consultants that presented information on the subject of corporate culture. An automobile-manufacturing executive told me that his firm paid over $3 million to a consulting firm to develop and define their corporate culture. I kidded with him by telling him I would do it for a lot less. In actuality, it would cost a fraction of what they paid if they were to follow the simple procedure of asking front-line employees the following questions:

1. How do they feel about working for the organization?

2. Are they proud of the company?

3. How do they feel about the way management treats them?

4. Do they think the company produces quality products/services?

5. Do they feel they are responsible for the quality of the products or services the organization offers?

6. Are the necessary support, encouragement, and resources made available to them to do a quality job?

Like it or not, their answers will define the basis of your company's corporate culture. *Your corporate culture is in the minds and actions of your employees.* It doesn't matter what you wish it to be, it is what it is. It's obvious that your front line will reflect the values and attitudes of their management. But, unless the managers act in accordance with the culture, the employees will not. They will tend toward mimicking the behavior of those who rule over them.

I DON'T OWN THE STORE

Consider the following example. Several years ago, I stopped by a popular fast-food restaurant in Ft. Lauderdale, Florida, because one of my children had to use the restroom. Upon entering the restroom I was shocked to see water on the floor, one sink not in order, broken toilet seats, and dirt everywhere. Figuring that I'd do the manager a favor, I went to the counter and pulled him aside to comment quietly on the condition of the restroom. He responded in a loud voice: "I just had a $300.00 order to fill and I'll get to the restrooms later." I saw that he was missing my point. It wasn't a simple matter of cleaning the restroom. I was complaining about my experience of his business and, because he was the manager, I was actually providing him with valuable information about his business.

I felt I was getting nowhere with the manager, so I asked him to give me the name of someone who would care about solving the problem. He abruptly turned away from me and began to walk into his office to get me a name. While on his way he looked at one of the workers at the grill and said, "All I need is this —hole tonight!" He said it loud enough so that a number of customers waiting in line heard it.

When he returned, he tossed a small piece of paper at me with only a telephone number on it. I immediately said that I didn't appreciate the profanity and now I was upset enough to bypass his store and call the chain's headquarters and complain. He said, "I don't care who you call, *I don't own the store.*"

Once he made that statement, I realized what the problem was. Here was a store manager who felt he had no responsibility to the customer because he didn't feel he had any ownership in the company. He considered the $300.00 order as an inconvenience, rather than a stroke of great luck. He also considered a complaint from a customer not important enough to warrant his immediate action. Because he felt no ownership or pride, his front line couldn't feel it.

The bottom line is that corporate culture is the way we act out our values within the organization. It is our actions and our ability to lead by example that will mold the experience of the employees and, in the long run, the customers. I am as totally convinced now as I was when I worked for Disney, that management must understand corporate culture if they want to change their organizations. It is only through understanding and appreciating the power of culture that change can occur in a lasting and orderly way.

KEY POINTS

1. Corporate culture represents the heart and soul of an organization. It consists of its values, traditions, and beliefs. Therefore, it is extremely important that management comprehensively understand corporate culture.
2. Corporate culture is the most difficult element of an organization to change.

3. Corporate culture is acted out by the front line of the organization and is therefore delivered to those outside for their interpretation.

4. Management must be committed to sustaining or changing corporate culture.

5. The common cultural element of all superior organizations is management caring about their employees. Management must have a sense of ownership and take responsibility for the actions of the company. Otherwise, it's highly unlikely that employees will feel a sense of ownership.

Chapter Seven

Staffing: Nonmanagement Personnel

Says Jim Poisant: In a competitive environment, service
is the only answer. He is right on target.
>   John Naisbitt, *Preparing Now for the Next Decade*

GOOD NEWS AND BAD NEWS

It goes without saying that people are the most important asset in any organization. Yet when it comes to selecting them, there is not a single test or interviewing technique that guarantees that the right personnel decision will be made. There are, however, several factors including the past work experience and the education of the prospective employee that increase the chances of hiring the right person for the job. Disney does a phenomenal job in recruiting people—perhaps the best in America when one considers the size, complexity, and success of their business.

In seeking to understand how Disney was so successful in hiring, I came by what appeared to be a contradiction in American corporate hiring practice. This was the practice of having prospective employees eliminate themselves from being hired by Disney. You read correctly, *eliminate* themselves. Disney staffing personnel conducted a preliminary interview that lasted between eight and ten minutes. The primary purpose of this brief interview was to make applicants aware of the negatives as well as the positives of working for Disney. It is assumed that prospective employees understand that working for Disney is a good career move; otherwise they wouldn't be applying. However, many applicants are not aware of the less-desirable aspects of working at Disney World. This simple technique could have outstanding results for you.

Think about what is going on in the mind of a typical person applying for a job. You've been there yourself. More than likely the applicant agrees with whatever the recruiter tells him or her just to get the job. However, when this happens the new hire must eventually deal with the company's policies, procedures, and job requirements. Before long, the individual may decide that the job is really not what he or she had in mind, so they quit or are let go. Before they leave, however, the organization has spent money, resources, and time to screen, hire, and train an individual that must be replaced.

When an applicant initially applies for an hourly position at Disney, they are met with a friendly smile and welcome. They are told that it is appreciated by the organization that they would consider working at Disney. Then the applicant is told about the grooming requirements for all employees. For example, there is a limitation on the number of rings that can be worn on each hand. Makeup has to be of natural color—no bright or excessive colors—and men's hair cannot cover their ears or touch their collar. They are told that Disney people work while other people play. In other words, it was highly likely that the applicant would work most holidays. After all, they will be working at the number-one vacation destination in the world and most people come during their vacation time. There is a limitation put on the size of earrings for women and, of course, men cannot wear earrings. Dark sunglasses are not allowed and only certain types and styles of footwear are authorized. Men are also not allowed to have any facial hair (there are exceptions to this rule). These possible negatively perceived requirements of working at Disney World are counterbalanced by the reputation of the company, the health benefits, discounts, and so on. Once the would-be employee completes the preorientation interview they are asked to come back within a few days for a second, more extensive interview lasting approximately 45 minutes.

You may be thinking that this procedure seems wasteful. Why not interview people and hire them if they meet the job requirements? The reason is simple. Some people, if given a few days to really think about the job requirements (both positive and negative), won't return for the next interview. These same people would more than likely leave the organization within the first few months either voluntarily or otherwise. Or worse, they may be disgruntled but may choose to stay with the organization. A Disney staffing person told me that the rate of "no returns" on the second interview was sometimes as high as 50 percent. Even if only 10–20 percent, it would be significant enough to warrant serious attention.

Do you have job requirements or company policies that new hires might not be aware of that may cause them to leave your organization? If you do, you may want to start conducting preemployment interviews. At the very least you will save time, money, and a lot of aggravation in the long run.

PEOPLE RECRUIT IN THEIR OWN IMAGE

Something I found particularly interesting was that the majority of the people Disney had doing their hiring were not career recruiters. They were not degreed professionals in the areas of Personnel or Human Resource Management. Instead, they were themselves recruited into staffing positions from within the Disney organization. Why? What could non-Human Resource employees possibly know about recruiting? The answer partially lies in the fact that by serving successfully in the company they knew better that anyone else what type of person could do their respective jobs. These "recruiters" not only did their jobs extremely well, but they also excelled in continuously modeling the corporate values and culture. This point is key because you ultimately want to hire people who will fit into and flourish within your culture. If new employees cannot adapt to the culture, you will end up with a minimum of four very unhappy parties: you, the employee, his or her peers, and your customers.

But is it enough just to have your best employees become your recruiters and let the rest just happen? Obviously anyone who is placed in a staffing position must be knowledgeable about how federal, state, and local laws apply to hiring people.

Knowing that staffing personnel were mostly recruited from within Disney helped me understand why the organization had such a good track record of retaining and motivating their employees. However, I didn't understand the true meaning of this practice until I had a conversation with the senior executive of the Human Resources Division of Disney World. His name is Jim. It turns out that Jim once worked with Walt Disney at Disneyland in California. Among a number of interesting tidbits about Disney staffing, he mentioned that many years ago Walt and his executives came to the conclusion that *people recruited in their own image.* I didn't understand the significance of his statement for a few days. Then it hit me like a ton of bricks: of course! What the recruiters were really doing was more *instinctive* than anything else. They were naturally drawn to the people who reflected their personal values and behaviors. Over time I have become more and more appreciative of the insight that Disney management had about human nature. People do tend to recruit in their own image.

I recalled the disastrous personnel choices that I had witnessed in past organizations. Some people were like fish out of water. It seemed everyone in the organization had the same impression. Everyone except the recruiters, that is. Typically, people who had never worked the jobs they were recruiting for had done the hiring. The recruiters were looking for people like themselves. No wonder the selections were so hit-and-miss! Who better to select a maintenance person, salesperson, or fireman other than individuals who have already had success doing the jobs? Yet even today in many organizations, we continue in the old tradition of having our personnel departments do the screening and hiring.

To test the validity of this practice, simply sit at a table with five to ten people and pick the one who could best do your job. I'll bet that you would pick the person who best reflects your values—the one you like the best. You just recruited in your own image.

PERSONAL JOB QUALIFICATIONS

Let's assume that the recruiters pick out the people who they *feel* could best do the jobs. The next thing that they need to do is to consider the job requirements and determine whether or not the candidate is physically and intellectually capable of performing them. It has always amazed me that when companies hire people for typing jobs they require a typing test to measure speed and accuracy. But when companies hire someone to work with money they don't require proof that the person can add.

I remember an incident at a well-known fast-food restaurant that illustrates this point. I do not recall exactly what I had ordered (something like a hamburger, coffee, and dessert). I gave the young lady at the counter a five dollar bill. Since modern cash registers are equipped with labeled buttons for each item on the menu and provide employees with the correct amount of change, they don't require an A in math to operate. Well, on this day, this young lady's register was not working. She went into a panic. She pulled out a piece of paper and began to simulate the process of addition and subtraction. She didn't have a clue. She began to randomly give me change hoping that I would correct her. When she reached $8.00 in change I finally asked her if that was my change or someone else's she was giving me. Knowing that she was in deep water, she acted out of desperation. She pushed her scrap piece of paper across the counter to me and told me to figure it out myself. At that point, the store manager approached and began to reprimand the employee in front of her peers and about 20 customers. But blaming the employee wasn't the answer. After all, she was not prepared for the job. But what was clear was the fact that even though the register was designed to be foolproof, individuals who deal with money should at least be able to do simple addition and subtraction.

Of course there are any number of external variables that impact an organization's ability to hire the right people. When Disney World opened there were 15 applicants for every job opening; I believe the current ratio is something closer to three people for every position. Having several people applying for one job allows recruiters to be more selective in their choices. But the depth of talent available in any given field makes a huge difference in the type of individual being hired. For example, in the information technology profession, there are thousands of openings going unfilled due to an untrained workforce. This scenario forces many organizations to export their work to other states or even to other countries. In some cases, unqualified people are hired and the company incurs greater costs for training and supervision.

Another factor in attracting good employees is the reputation of your organization. If you are well known as a good place to work you will obviously have more applicants. It all stems from treating people with dignity and respect.

KEY POINTS

1. *Conduct an initial brief interview for all nonsupervisory job applicants.* During this initial interview explain the highlights of working for the company. This time should also be used to explain the downside of the job, such as dress code, working hours, and other requirements that may cause a person to become unmotivated or discontented.

2. *People tend to recruit in their own image.* The people you assign to do your recruiting should not only be familiar with job requirements but should have excelled in the positions they are recruiting for, not only technically but culturally. They should be your best examples of the behavior you most desire from employees.

3. *Make sure you hire people who can successfully complete the functions of the job.* You need to make sure that people can physically and intellectually do the jobs you are hiring them for. Simple tests and questions before you hire or place people may save your organization and its employees unnecessary grief.

4. *Do not relax your standards*. The day you decide to relax your standards is the day you lose your standards.

5. *If your organization is known as a good place to work, more applicants will apply*. The only way this will occur is if management treats their employees with dignity and respect.

Chapter Eight

Selecting Management

Wherever man goes to dwell, his character goes with
him.

African Proverb

THE CULTURAL INFLUENCE

Selecting individuals to manage organizations ranks as one of the
most, if not *the* most, important decisions organizations make.
Wrong decisions can sometimes cripple or destroy an organization.
Right decisions often lift organizations to greater heights. Managers
set examples for others to follow. They are most responsible for reinforcing the culture of an organization. They reward, motivate, and
discipline employees and they influence how the organization allo-
cates its human and physical resources. They are the people most responsible for the successes and failures of the organization.

It would be misleading to address the subject of management
selection without first considering the culture of an organization. I
have mentioned that hierarchical organizations tend to value different "strengths" of managers than circular (customer-focused)
organizations. Therefore, the *success criteria* for management are defined by the culture of each organization. The following illustrates a

subtle difference between hierarchical and customer-focused organizations.

During numerous speeches given over the years to thousands of executives and managers, I've asked this question. "If a man working in a hierarchical organization is observed crying at work, what would others consider his promotion potential to be?" The immediate reaction from audiences is that the person is weak and more than likely would not be chosen for promotion. This reaction was nearly unanimous. No one had asked me to tell them the reason why he was crying. The mere fact that he was weeping was enough to doom him.

When the same audience was asked about a man crying in a customer-focused organization, the responses were much different. Audiences were much more compassionate. Instead of dooming him, they wanted to know why he was crying. When asked about women crying in hierarchical organizations both male and female managers had the same response. They felt that it was more understandable for women rather than men to be crying. However, their fate was the same. They would more than likely not be promoted because they were perceived as being weak.

For those who think that people who show emotion and compassion in business do not succeed, answer this question. "Who would you prefer to work for, a person who shows emotion or one who doesn't?" Unless the manager comes from a different planet, he or she feels emotion. My firsthand experience and research over decades has taught me that executives in excellent service organizations are not ashamed to show emotion and compassion. It all depends on how you and the organization define "strength."

SENIOR MANAGEMENT

Organizations are often faced with the difficult decision of hiring from within or going outside to recruit senior executives. When selections come from within there is general knowledge of how the individual being promoted will act in given situations. That's the good news. The bad news is the same person probably would not bring fresh ideas or change to the organization. Additionally, if an organization chooses to go outside, more than likely there will be animosity from some of those who were passed over.

Perhaps you are wondering if it's better to stay inside or venture out. In their 1994 book, *Built to Last: Successful Habits of Visionary Companies*, James C. Collins and Jerry I. Porras said that going inside for a CEO position might very well be the smartest thing to do. "In seventeen *hundred* years of combined life spans across the visionary companies, we found only four individual incidents of going outside for a CEO—and those in only two companies" (p. 18). Maybe there is a lesson to be learned here.

AVOIDING THE "PETER PRINCIPLE"

The *Peter Principle* is defined as "the notion that an employee within an organization will advance to his highest level of incompetence and remain there" (*American Heritage Dictionary*, 1985, p. 927). I agree with this so-called principle. There are vast numbers of people who, if given the opportunity, resources, and mentoring, would not ever qualify as being incompetent. However, many people are promoted to these so-called positions of incompetence who should not have been promoted in the first place. People get promoted for a number of reasons. Their dad may own the company or they use politics to work their way up the ladder. In a vast number of cases, however, organizations promote people into management positions because they fit the culture and are successful individual performers. Success as an individual performer does not necessarily equate to success as a manager of people.

The reason is simple. The aptitude and skills required to manage people are quite different from those of managing oneself. In sales, for example, outstanding salespeople are often promoted to sales management positions. Unfortunately this promotion practice creates a double-edged sword. On one side, organizations often lose their best salespeople. On the other side, the organization gets hurt because of inept managers. This situation duplicates itself in all areas of organizations from sales to operations. Just because a person knows how machines work does not mean he should become the shop manager.

It may sound odd, but the truth is that many people who are successful in their nonmanagerial jobs do not really want to be managers. Often, these individuals find themselves in a bind. They are never quite comfortable with the process of making things run smoothly by motivating others. After they receive the promotion, a new title, and more money, they discover that they are a counselor, a coach, a motivational expert, a financial advisor, and a psychologist. They often complain that the more they do for their employees, the more they are expected to do. Where they once had a job that had a finitely defined scope of responsibility, they now have what they perceive to be a sprawling mass of unending hats to wear. They find themselves having to please employees in addition to customers and management. In a number of cases, individuals find themselves so frustrated that they blame their ineffectiveness on their employees.

These individuals find it very difficult to admit that they do not know how to manage. The result is that those who don't want to—or simply can't—manage people find themselves stuck in management positions. Some even regard their very roles as managers to be some sort of punishment.

This situation of having individual performers "rewarded" by giving them management jobs is a blatant example of why hierarchically run organizations find it so difficult to create and sustain superior customer service. *The emphasis in hierarchical organizations is on moving up in the organization versus moving toward the customer.*

THE SELECTION PROCESS

As stated, poor management selections run the risk of doing serious damage to organizations. The damage could vary widely. Let's assume that you are a manager in an organization that has a reputation for being a great place to work. There has been a friendly, team-oriented environment in place since the company was founded. There is no intention of changing it. However, the company had grown to the point where you need to go outside for management talent. An outside executive recruiting firm or head-hunter is called in to assist in the search. A typical process of hiring goes something like this: you review the list of qualified candidates, set up a series of interviews, and the candidates parade through your organization one at a time. Each meets with the senior managers of the organization, perhaps goes to lunch with one or two executives, and then returns home.

After the interviews, you call for a discussion and a vote. One male candidate stands out among the rest. His background information checks out. He said all the right things and looked the part of someone who would represent your company well. You extend the offer, the person accepts, and the sometimes very expensive process of relocating the person and their family begins. Within 30 days of hiring the new executive you begin to hear rumblings that your "wonderful" choice is singlehandedly destroying the organization's family-type environment that took so long to establish. He is intimidating his staff and threatening to fire employees who question his authority. He tells employees that they should distrust customers and they should question everything the customers say and do. You have a crisis on your hands. You either have to give this guy a lobotomy or you have to get rid of him. As bad as this guy is you feel that there is no way to "save" him. You simply made a mistake. Unfortunately this scene is repeated time and time again. In a number of cases the organization doesn't replace the person. They either don't want to admit they made a mistake or they don't want to go through the process again.

A well-publicized case of selecting the wrong executive for a senior management job happened in the mid-nineties to none other than the Walt Disney Company. After the untimely death of Disney's President Frank Wells, Disney's Chairman Michael Eisner set out to fill the vacant post from outside Disney. Infuriated over this decision, one senior Disney executive departed under less-than-friendly terms and began another company to compete against Disney. The man chosen for the job was one of the most powerful people in Hollywood. Unfortunately, he was the wrong guy for the job. One year later he received a severance package worth millions of dollars. Disney ultimately felt that the extraordinary payment was less expensive compared to the potential long-term damage of keeping him in such a vital position. This story repeats itself time after time and everyone loses, including the customer.

To date, there are no foolproof ways of selecting the "right" executives and managers. No aptitude tests, no quick screening tools, no guarantees. However, there are a few things to keep in mind that should improve the probability. The first thing to consider is the entire process of selection. If the selection process as I have described it is one that your organization practices with hit-or-miss results, then maybe it is the process.

I cannot prescribe the exact steps an organization must take to increase their chances of making the right selection decisions. However, I can recommend a reexamination of the organization's selection measurement criteria. The foremost criterion for selection is that management must *know* the person they are hiring. This is difficult. In most organizations managers do not really know the people who have worked for them for years. So even suggesting the idea that they know people before they hire them is radical. Most hiring managers are satisfied with a resumé, background check, and interviews. Few take the time to really get to know the person. I can't say how long that process will take or the exact way to do it: the answer lies within the person(s) responsible for the hiring. Getting to know people might sound costly and timely. If you think it is, think about the real cost of making the wrong decision.

KNOWING THE APPLICANT

The central issue in hiring management from outside is whether or not the executive will assimilate into and benefit the culture of the organization. I recognize that in some cases, executives are chosen to assist in changing cultures. When this happens the organization is usually in serious trouble financially.

In addition to the applicant's resumé and the advice of the recruiters, there are a number of other factors to consider. Has the applicant demonstrated the ability to manage and motivate people? The applicant will say that he or she is very good at doing whatever they need to do to impress the interviewer. This is human nature. What is wrong with asking the people who had firsthand experience of working for the applicant? How badly does the applicant want the job? How persistent has he or she been? Is this the first time the individual has expressed an interest in the company? Find out! Did the applicant send thank you notes back to those with whom or he or she interviewed? Did he or she recognize the administrative assistants and secretaries and thank them? Has the individual taken the time and put forth the effort to understand the company history? There are several sources to get information about an organization. There is little excuse for a senior management applicant not doing his or her homework. The reason I am stressing this particular aspect is simple. If the person has voluntarily learned a great deal about your organization, there is an excellent chance that they are truly interested in becoming a contributing member.

Disney vividly drove this point home to me during my own recruitment process. After several months, scores of interviews, and three trips from Miami to Orlando, I was confident I would be selected to head the company's new Business Seminar Division. Finally I got the phone call I was waiting for from Disney. I thought it strange that the executive recruiter asked me if I had another job offer? I said I did not. Then he said something I will never forget, "Well, if you do have another offer *take it.*" This comment took me by total surprise!

"Take it," I replied, "you mean I do not have the job at Disney?" You have to appreciate the fact that I was positive I had the job. I told him that even if I had another offer, I would wait to hear from Disney before I did anything. Then he said something even more peculiar. "Jim, that was the answer I was looking for, you're hired!"

Although I was pleased to get the job, I was upset that he appeared to be playing games with something very important to me—my livelihood. A few weeks after being hired, I got the chance to pull him aside and asked what the purpose of the telephone call was. He said it was simple. "Our experience when hiring executives from the outside is that the ones who make it with Disney really want to be here," he said. "We've found that the people who really want to work for the organization tend to learn faster and assimilate into the culture faster." He was right.

Although there are no hard and fast rules, it is important to spend a considerable amount of time with prospective executives. The typical one hour with several executives giving their "blessing" or rejecting the person is not enough time to assess cultural kinship. Days are more like it. Get to know the person. Do not talk about work, talk about life in general and spend time in informal settings. How often does he or she mention family? Does he or she listen sincerely? Ask him or her what they would do in particular situations. Really get to know the person you plan on putting in charge.

One direct benefit your organization derives from recruiting an individual who has a tremendous desire to be part of the team is that in all probability the individual will seek to understand everything they can about the organization on their own as well as through training. They will learn rapidly and therefore be of greater benefit to the organization in a shorter amount of time.

When it comes to selecting the right executive, the "real person" is discovered only over time. They either live up to or exceed expectations or they don't. Therefore, spend an ample amount of time with your top candidates before you hire them. It's much less expensive and painful for everyone.

Last but not least, include your employees in decision making in the hiring process. How do they feel about this new person? If it is true that people recruit in their own image, ask the people in your organization about how they feel about prospective candidates. If they think the person will be an asset, they will tell you. If they don't, they will tell you that as well.

KEY POINTS

1. An organization's culture determines the criteria for success as managers. Hierarchical (top-down) organizations tend to dis-

play different values than circular (customer-driven) organizations. Making the right selection of management personnel is crucial to any organization. Managers set examples for others to follow. They are the ones most responsible for the successes and failures of the organization.

2. When organizations choose from within their ranks for managers there is less risk of making a mistake. On the other had, it's unlikely that the organization will benefit from the new ideas and contacts the outside executive brings.

3. In many cases people chosen for management positions from inside an organization are selected mainly because they performed well as individuals. The skills it takes to be an effective manager are quite different from those of an individual performer. Many people promoted to management positions feel that they are being punished.

4. The most important aspect of hiring a manager from outside the organization is how well the person will reflect the organization's corporate culture.

5. Organizations hiring managers and executives from outside must establish a selection process that allows the organization to know the real person, not the job seeker. *Do not* hire managers just to fill slots. The time, energy, and true costs of failure need to be considered.

6. Ask those who will be working with or for the prospective new hire how they feel about the person being considered. Their votes count.

Chapter Nine

Training, Culture, and the Organization

A company that has a well-defined customer focus and that successfully manages the knowledge gained through incremental improvements is much more likely to trigger innovation than is an organization that is satisfied with the status quo.

W. Edwards Deming
Andrea Gabor, *The Man Who Discovered Quality*

THE STATE OF EDUCATION

It is widely recognized that the U.S. educational system is in a great deal of trouble. So much so that education reform was one of the main issues in the 2000 presidential campaign. Each year tens of thousands of students either drop out or graduate from schools ill prepared to enter the workforce. Many lack even the basic skills of reading, mathematics, and writing. Yet a diploma from a college or university in the United States is highly valued in other countries. More confounding is the fact that U.S. companies are hiring workers from outside the United States to fill job vacancies.

It would be folly to think that there is no correlation between the level of education and a person's ability to perform on a job. It would also be folly for those in management to count on the formal education system to improve enough for companies not to be concerned about training their employees.

The fact is that businesses continue to spend millions of dollars each year filling in the gaps created by an outdated educational system. These gaps are widening due to rapid technological advances. Few educational institutions can keep up with the cost of purchasing leading-edge technologies and recruiting and retaining corresponding faculty. Conversely, teachers with technical skills are being recruited to the private sector. To further complicate matters, a strong economy makes human resources hard to come by; skilled workers are extremely difficult to find.

So if you're in management, what does the state of formal education mean to you? Simply put, it means that the ball is in your court. Organizations must be able to make up for the deficiencies in their employees' education in order to maximize their value to the organization.

TWO MAJOR FUNCTIONS OF TRAINING

Organizational training serves two separate, but related functions. The first is *cultural*—the teaching of corporate values, traditions, and behaviors. The second is to teach specific, *job-related* skills. While the second is the one most associated with corporate training, most organizations underestimate the importance of the first function—cultural training. As you know, I dedicated an entire chapter to the subject of corporate culture. If corporate culture is understood it can be facilitated and reinforced through the training process.

Whenever I review organizational training programs, I observe an interesting commonality in their design. The majority of businesses provide new employees with some sort of orientation training and some continuing education that occurs randomly during their time with the organization. Few organizations, however, view the training of employees in a planned, systematic way, and even fewer do so in an approach that spans their careers with the company.

THE EMPLOYEE ORIENTATION PROCESS

Employees' experience with a company begins before they work a single day. In many cases, prospective employees are well aware of an organization's reputation. The better the reputation, the more appealing the organization is for potential employees. The interview process is typically the first formal opportunity an employer has to provide a positive experience for a potential employee.

There are several things that employers can do to make prospective employees feel welcome. The way an applicant is greeted, interviewed, and thanked will form impressions about the organization.

Once hired, the formal orientation process provides an excellent opportunity for organizations to provide everyone the same information about the organization's values, traditions, and history. It is highly recommended that company employees who *exemplify the company's ideals* conduct the new employee orientation program, and that new employee orientation occurs *before* any new hire is allowed to report to work.

If new hires report directly to the workplace without going through a formal orientation program, their job becomes their orientation. The organization misses the only opportunity it has to share its vision. As I surveyed organizations I found that most miss out on the tremendous benefits of well-designed orientation programs. They either do not use them to reinforce their corporate culture and/or they do not require new hires to go through orientation before they report to their jobs. This is a great loss to the company as well as the employees.

ESSENTIALS OF ORIENTATION PROGRAMS

When designing or reviewing existing orientation programs, it is important to recognize that these programs are *extremely important*. As mentioned, they provide organizations with a unique opportunity to instill the values, traditions, and practices of organizations.

Outstanding orientation programs that I observed over a number of years contained the following ten basic elements:

1. Present the history and traditions of your organization
2. Explain the mission and vision of the organization
3. Spell out employer expectations
4. Create a team spirit among new employees
5. Enhance the self-image of new employees
6. Reward and discipline guidelines
7. Communicate administrative issues such as employee benefits
8. Review safety procedures, as appropriate
9. Answer questions new employees might have
10. Provide a tour of buildings, cafeterias, the mailroom, and so on

The lengths of these programs vary, but for the most part last only a few days. Once employees complete their orientation, it is critical that the information and values they were given be reinforced throughout their stay with the organization.

DESIGN AROUND DIFFERENCES

Here is something to think about when designing training programs: few consider the fact that people have different interests based on their age and generations. For example, a person born in the 1950s has a different set of experiences and influences than a person born in the eighties or nineties. They have experienced different music, different heroes, and different economic cycles (recession, inflation, low employment). These differences have an impact on the way people perceive information. Yet if you go into corporate classrooms today, you will more than likely find training being presented without these individual distinctions being considered.

Having a training program that, by design, considers each employee's educational and work-related psychological needs from orientation to retirement provides numerous benefits to your employees and your company. While most organizations recognize the need to provide training at the beginning of an employees career, few provide planned training throughout their careers. There are exceptions, typically in technical fields such as engineering and medicine, where constant training is required. But the training I am referring to addresses the person's individual and professional needs.

Recognizing that people's needs change all the time, Disney puts a great deal of emphasis on training throughout the careers of their employees. Unless it has changed since I was a cast member, the Human Resources Division was decentralized to meet the particular needs of the workers in different areas of the company. For example, hotel/resort division workers had different needs than those who worked in theme parks. But in every case the overriding goal of training was to reinforce and perpetuate the values of the company.

There are several times when training can be systematically provided throughout a person's career. Obviously each organization will have its own particular requirements. But as you assess your own you will discover that there are similarities in every organization. One that spans virtually every company is the need to provide information on retirement. I recognize that in today's society life-long employment with one organization is rare. However, organizations need to provide such information as part of their overall strategy for motivating employees.

In order to design a training program for those approaching retirement, the curriculum developers would have to perform a needs assessment as part of their research. Obviously, one of the biggest concerns a would-be retiree could have is his or her retirement and pension benefit. How can they continue to receive health benefits? What about life insurance? Is there any assistance in estate and tax planning? Despite their differences, every training program contains people with common needs. With the exception of military organizations, I am not aware of any organization that is known for its "cradle to grave" training programs. What I am advocating is for managers to understand that people have common and unique training requirements.

Your challenge then is to examine your organization's training programs to see if they address your employees' educational and personal needs over time. I recommend that you construct your own model training chart. Plot your existing training, and then impose the appropriate additional training along the chart line. Keep in mind that your overall program will take time to establish and that it will require changes over time. Remember that your overall goal with training, as well as most everything else you do, is to provide a nurturing, caring environment for your employees so that your customers' experiences are positive.

TRAINERS/COURSE DESIGNERS

To make sure your training program is effective, consider these points: First, *don't* have your most expendable people teach. Instead, have your best do the teaching. This only makes common sense because students know who to listen to and they appreciate learning from those who have "been there." When it comes to designing the curriculum, make sure that the people who know the jobs best are involved. Training is too important and expensive to not get the right material taught by the right people. These practices will pay off immensely. Finally, before you allow a new course or seminar to be offered, make sure the first class consists of people who have experienced what you are about to teach. In other words, let this group serve as a focus group. I guarantee they will produce a number of concrete, useful suggestions that can be incorporated into the curriculum.

THE GREEN BERETS ARRIVE

It matters very little if you have the most elaborate, well-designed training program in the world if those receiving the training cannot perform their jobs correctly. I learned this lesson the hard way, through the school of hard knocks.

In the mid-seventies, I directed the training division for The Wackenhut Corporation, a private security and investigative firm headquartered in Coral Gables, Florida. At the time, the company had approximately 22,000 employees. The company had won its largest contract in its history, referred to as the Savanna River Plant. This particular contract required security protection for a number of "top secret"facilities that produced tritium (a rare radioactive hydrogen isotope with atomic mass used as the trigger mechanism for nuclear weapons). Protection of such an important facility required a very high level of security. As director of training, I had the overall responsibility to make sure that all of the 700 employees assigned to the project were properly trained.

Wackenhut was not unfamiliar with how to train and protect nuclear weapons facilities. It had been providing security at the Nevada Test Site for several years prior to winning the Savanna River Plant contract, but the security required for the new contract had many unique requirements. At the Nevada site, weapons were transported from production facilities around the country to the desert test areas and exploded. The Savanna River site was far more complex because there were five nuclear plants, plus a number of other vital facilities contributing to the production of tritium.

There were several hundred security officers who had to be trained. Each had to go through a rigid screening process with preference given to those with prior police or military experience. Regardless of their previous experience, every new hire was required to go through weeks of academic, physical, and weapons training. On paper, these "troops" looked very well trained. However, after the first few classes reported to their posts I had an uneasy feeling about the readiness of the force. I knew that there would be attempts by U.S. military Special Forces (Green Berets) to test our security. And even thought the guard force "passed" all the training requirements, I was not absolutely convinced we were ready to repel the U.S. military.

It was Thanksgiving night when I visited several security officers at their guard posts to say hello. One particular post was located in the middle of a field between one of the nuclear plants and the perimeter fence. That night I made a very disturbing discovery.

As we talked about the training they received I asked them what they would do if the bad guys began an attack. All three officers gave me textbook answers. Then I asked them to act as if we were really under attack.

What I witnessed was not a pretty sight. There was total confusion as everyone went in different directions and hid behind barriers that could not protect them against the types of weapons a terrorist would use. What was painfully obvious was that with all the training they received, they couldn't put it all together. It was at that point I learned that training was incomplete unless the students actually demonstrated they understood what was taught. A student could get an A on an exam and even act out what they were taught, but it was useless unless they could put all of the lessons together to produce the expected results.

The next day I called the training staff together to discuss our situation. The entire curriculum had to be revised. The new one combined scenario training. We called it "what if" training. We would dream up things the "bad guys" might do and come up with ways to counter them. When the mock attacks came, we were successful. I believe to this day that we wouldn't have been able to stop the Green Berets if we didn't really test our students.

The lesson to be learned is not to take anything for granted when you train someone. Have students actually perform the functions you are training them for.

KEY POINTS

1. The educational system in the United States falls short of providing skilled, well-prepared workers to fill U.S workforce requirements.

2. Organizations, not school systems, are responsible for corporate values training.

3. The two main functions of corporate training are to teach values and job-related skills.

4. Organizations typically provide some form of new employee orientation and random continuing education.

5. Employees who best exemplify the values of the organization should teach orientation programs.

6. New employee orientation should take place before a new hire is allowed to report to their job.

7. Effective orientation programs consist of ten basic elements.

8. Generational differences should be considered when training programs are being designed.

9. Training programs should be designed to meet the needs of employees throughout their careers.

10. The people chosen to design training programs should be those who best know the subject matter, those who work with the contents of the training.

11. The true test of training is performance. If a person cannot perform what they were taught, then they were not taught well enough.

Chapter Ten

Effective Organizational Communication

The power of words is immense. A well-chosen word has often sufficed to stop a flying army, to change defeat into victory, and to save an empire.

Emile De Feather

Ted Goodman, *Forbes Book of Business Quotations*

FORMS OF COMMUNICATION

The quest for creating and sustaining a superior customer service organization depends directly on management's ability to effectively communicate inside as well as outside the organization. A number of research studies have indicated that the majority of organizational problems are directly or indirectly related to communication. Yet so little is understood about how to effectively communicate. Before we can hope to benefit from effectively using communication, it is important to understand that organizational communication comes in many forms: executive behavior, speeches, memoranda, letters, newsletters, bulletin boards, special announcements, corporate events, corporate values statements, mission statements, annual reports, films, news reports, training courses, the look of the physical environment, signage, policies, procedures, and last but not least the company grapevine.

Typically, communication occurs within organizations with little or no overall purpose other than to simply pass information along. Excellent service organizations, however, intentionally use communication to reinforce their corporate values.

ACTION STEPS FOR MANAGEMENT

In order to create and sustain a superior customer service organization, management needs to:

1. Recognize that all forms of communication within the organization, in addition to simply transmitting and receiving information, perpetuate the culture of the organization.
2. Review each type of communication to ensure that each contributes to reinforcing the values of the organization.
3. Appoint a person who best reflects the organization's culture to periodically review communication elements of the organization.

To implement these recommended actions, begin by identifying every method of communication being used within your organization. A good starting point is to take a sample of each piece of print material and lay them out before you. Do they reflect a consistent look? Do they reflect the values of your organization? What kind of mood or feeling do they give? Are they reflective of the level of quality you wish to see?

Chances are they were not designed with these elements in mind. Most likely they were designed/written by a variety of people who simply wanted to deliver information to their intended audiences. There was probably little attention paid to how each piece of material compared to other pieces. Your task is to break down each piece of written material to assess the number of different messages they give to the reader. For example, look at the percentage of administrative versus employee-focused information they contain. Are they consistent? Do they look like they came from the same place, and most important, do they articulate, relate, or reinforce the culture of your organization?

Once you do the breakdown and access the status of the communication system, you'll need to set guidelines for future publications in terms of both form and content. But before you establish this overall direction, you will need to determine what messages you wish to put forth. (*Refer back to your mission.*) Let's say that you want to distribute messages regarding the importance of friendliness and quality customer service. The most effective way that I have seen is placing great emphasis on rewarding behavior of those who render outstanding customer service. Employees appear in newsletters receiving plaques and other awards for jobs well done.

COMMUNICATING THROUGH THE ENVIRONMENT

The next part of your communication system is the one that is usually most overlooked—the physical environment. Lobbies, cafeterias, hallways, restrooms, roads, factory floors, parking lots, administrative areas, offices, break areas, art work, and signage all make up the physical environment of your organization. How are the cafeterias decorated? Do they appear warm and welcoming? How are the general conditions of the buildings and grounds? Is there any trash on the ground? What kinds of messages are being sent out to employees and visitors? If the employee work or rest areas are unclean, do not expect your employees to care about cleanliness of the customer areas/products.

Signs are a powerful way to communicate. They can send positive (promoting the culture) or negative messages. Signs that say NO SMOKING or PARK HERE versus PLEASE DO NOT SMOKE or PLEASE PARK HERE are subtle but different ways of sending the same messages.

In the early nineties, I had the pleasure of addressing approximately 600 employees at the New England Exposition in Springfield, Massachusetts, on the subject of quality customer service.

Known as the BIG "E" and held each year in late September, over 1 million people visit the exposition in just 12 days. Before my speech, I toured the grounds of the exposition with one of the BIG "E" senior managers. I asked her to join me in looking at the grounds and facilities from the customers' eyes. It wasn't long before we picked out a sign that conveyed a negative message. One of the food stands had a very large sign right in the middle of it that read, ID REQUIRED—MUST BE SHOWN. In reality, over 99.9 percent of the guests would not be trying to break the law, yet everyone would be subjected to this negative message.

Look at your signage to see what messages they really convey. Ask your employees to suggest more positive ways to reflect a superior service image through signage. If you think that I'm going too far with this issue, good. You are beginning to understand what it will really take to create and sustain a superior customer service organization. As Carl Sewell says in his book *Customers for Life*, "Signs are a subtle way to tell the world what your values are and what kind of business you are running. Since that's true, do them right" (1990, p. 124).

EXECUTIVE MODELING

Regardless of what your written communications say, you cannot hope to have an effective communication system unless the most important part of the system is working at all times. If you haven't guessed by now, the most important part of the communication system is executive behavior. I will refer to this behavior as *modeling* because employees typically model the behavior of their management. *The executive and management staff must embody the values of the company in everything they say and do.* Achieving this will be a continuing challenge, because it requires many managers to change their behavior.

Respected managers are coaches, not bosses. Where do your executives eat, among themselves or with employees? If they eat in the employee cafeteria, where do they sit and with whom? In many organizations, I have observed "special" tables used only by managers. The tables aren't marked "reserved for special people," though it's common knowledge that they say "Do not sit here unless you are an executive or everyone in the cafeteria will glare at you." Where do your executives park? Where do they spend their time during working hours? In their offices or out with employees? You determine what kind of messages your employees are receiving by observing the behavior of your managers and executives.

CONSTANT MONITORING AND QUALITY CONTROL

Your communication system will require constant monitoring and adjusting. It will be necessary to survey employees and customers continually. It will also be necessary to be honest when presenting information. People will trust what you say if you are up-front and honest with them; they can handle the bad as well as the good news.

Remember the importance of an effective communication system. Not only will it help you to reduce organizational problems; it is also vital for your organization in order to render and sustain superior service. I cannot overemphasize this fact. People need to know what is expected of them. An effective communication system is the only way to guide them. Don't forget how important it is to have management and leadership modeling the values of the organization.

KEY POINTS

1. The underlying goal of effective communication is to reinforce the culture of the organization.

2. All elements that make up organizational communication must be reviewed and must align with the organization's mission and values.

3. The communication system contains a number of different mediums including written and verbal communication.

4. Employees who exemplify the corporate values must be publicly and privately recognized and rewarded. This recognition must be embedded in the culture so that all employees know what management values in their behavior.

5. The physical environment of an organization offers a wonderfully powerful way to communicate the values of the organization.

6. Executive and management staff must model the values of the organization at all times. Failure to do so is damaging, if not deadly, to achieving and sustaining superior customer service.

7. Communication systems require constant monitoring and adjustment.

Chapter Eleven

The Untapped Power of Language

The secret of success—or failure, for that matter—is that
we become what we think about.
　　Earl Nightingale, *Earl Nightingale's Greatest Discovery*

DISCOVERING A SUPERIOR CUSTOMER SERVICE VOCABULARY

If, in fact, we are what we think, then it stands to reason that the language we use to express our thoughts is extremely important. Your ability to offer superior customer service and products will be enhanced dramatically when you tap into the tremendous power of language.

Before joining Disney I must admit I really didn't appreciate how much langauge impacts our daily life. When used properly, words can be a very powerful asset for organizations. They cause actions, give impressions, and convey moods and feelings. Words can be used to motivate, intimidate, reward, or punish.

Shortly after arriving at Disney I was taken with what amounted to be a new vocabulary called "Disneyese." Over time I figured out that early in the establishment of the culture, Disney management intentionally adopted words and terms to reinforce the values of the organization.

"DISNEYESE"

Among the most powerful words is "Guest." The word "Guest" (with a capital G) is used in place of the word "customer." It was obvious to me that Disney management wanted to ensure that their employees would render outstanding cutomer service. What better way of convincing them by having them believe that they were serving Guests versus customers? If you doubt how subtly powerful this distinction is, just imagine the treatment customers would get in everyday business transactions on retail floors, in reception areas, or on the Internet if the people serving the customers *really believed* that customers were "guests." Disney management went one step further and added the notion that their customers were not only Guests—but special Guests within the employees' homes (Disney parks). The results for Disney continue to be astounding. Disney is legendary in the area of customer service. It stands to reason that customers who are treated as special guests in someone's home want to return. It is no surprise that Disney has an extremely high rate of return business.

Another very important use of words is the term "cast member," which is used in lieu of employees. Everyone from security guards and ride operators to maids and senior management is referred to as a cast member. Disney employees are taught early on that every cast member has an important role within the organization. Every employee contributes to what the guests experience. This in itself is motivational. To the contrary, there are millions of workers who go to work each day not knowing how they fit into the overall scheme of the organization. It is little wonder why many of these workers are not highly motivated. The term cast member also aids in the elimination of the tendency to stereotype people by their job titles. Let's face it, we live in a world that values titles. In excellent service organizations the value is on customer service, not titles.

While I'm not suggesting that all employees be called cast members, I am suggesting that organizations stop calling them employees or workers and find a name that is both positive and appropriate to the business. The late Sam Walton, founder of Wal-Mart, called his employees "associates." It certainly worked for him.

Other words used in the Disney vocabulary also had and continue to have a powerful impact on people's perception of themselves, their responsibilities, their customers, and the company's culture. You will notice in the following additional examples of "Disneyese" that there is a deliberate attempt by management to use language to guide the behavior of the organization.

Host or Hostess: In addition to being called a cast member, each person employed at a Disney theme park is referred to as a host or hostess. There are hundreds of job descriptions, but only one job title for everyone. They are either a host or hostess to their guests.

Show: Since Disney is in the entertainment business, the show is basically anything the guests experience. This includes the way they are treated by the cast, live entertainment, attractions, food service, as well as the physical environment. The word "show" is used to reinforce the idea that the entire guest experience is a show and everything that is said and done by the organization contributes to the show.

Good Show/Bad Show: These terms are used to describe the quality of the show (the guest's experience). If every aspect of a performance, attraction, service, or speech were not up to Disney's standards of high quality it would be referred to as "bad show." On the other hand, if the guest's experience met Disney standards it would be referred to as "good show." These words are used to emphasize the fact that the guest's experience is based on his or her total experience—"the show."

On Stage: Defined as any area where guests are found. The significance of this term is to reinforce the need for cast members to act as if they were on stage in front of the guests.

Off Stage: Refers to areas where guests would not be found. Cast members can relax, and be out of costume in these areas.

Costumes: Clothing worn by cast members. Because each cast member has a particular role to play in the "show," they need to wear appropriate costumes. Regardless of their job function, whether it is sweeping the streets or dressing up as Snow White, costumes are of equal importance, both off stage and on stage.

Setting: When Walt Disney produced films he was able to approve each word and visual before the paying audience ever saw the production. When he built his first park, Disneyland, however, he had a much greater challenge. He needed to control the setting as much as possible so the guests would be able to fully enjoy the parks. He knew that it only took one thing to be out of place to ruin the setting. The setting is anything the guests see and experience.

It didn't take me long to observe that anything that appeared to be out of place on stage attracted the attention of the guests. Trash is perhaps the best example. If a piece of paper or a soda were on the ground, guests would immediately notice it. While their attention is drawn to the trash their impression of the setting is diminished. This would be an example of "bad show."

First Names: My personal favorite when it comes to the effective use of language is the use of first names. Several senior Disney managers would tell me that they thought calling cast members by their first names was the most important tradition the company had. It was amazing to watch the interaction between people because they could call each other by name. Each person within the Disney guest area wears a name badge with only their first name printed in large letters. The letters are large enough to be seen at a distance, which allows you to get over the somewhat uncomfortable feeling that occurs when you forget someone's name. It also breaks down the interpersonal barriers caused by rank and status. When you feel free to call the president by his or her first name, it creates an informal atmosphere, which benefits the organization immeasurably. Just the fact that management personnel feel comfortable with using first names is a giant step toward creating a highly productive, less stressful environment.

Plusing the Show: This term refers simply to making something better than it is. I have a vivid memory of "Plusing the Show" at Disney. My peers would give me their recommendations as to how I could improve my presentations. The thing that amazed me the most was the nonthreatening environment that existed in order to allow everyone involved to concentrate on doing a better job. After every presentation, no matter how successful, I would review my performance (the show) to see how I could "plus it." Several times my co-workers (audiovisual crew, course designers) would offer a critique of my work. If you can make plusing the show a way of life in your organization, two things will happen: the quality of your products and services will be improved, and you will create a sense of pride in your employees that will pay short- and long-term dividends.

Aggressively Friendly: This term is used to punctuate the need for every cast member to be outwardly friendly to the guests. It is not enough to be just friendly. Cast members should feel empowered to be "aggressively" friendly. To some people being openly friendly comes naturally. For others there needs to be encouragement and sound rationale behind changing their behavior. Consider the classic scenario of a family member taking pictures of his or her family while on vacation. This situation presents a great opportunity to be aggressively friendly by volunteering to take the picture. Once the family returns home, chances are they will remember that nice preson (as well as the organization) who took the picture of their entire family. After all, it will probably be the only picture of all of them they have. Being aggressively or openly friendly has its rewards to the business, the customers and the employees.

AGGRESSIVELY FRIENDLY IN TAIWAN

My favorite example of the power of the term aggressively friendly occurred in Taiwan in June 2000. I had the distinction of being the International Executive Director for the 2000 World Congress on Information Technology. This event began in 1978 and has moved from country to country every two years since then. This congress is a very high-profile event for the host country. The program inluded the newly elected president of Taiwan, Bill Gates (Microsoft), John Chambers (Cisco), Carly Fiorina (Hewlett Packard), a Nobel prizewinner, and scores of other notables. I was asked to take part in training of the hundreds of young student volunteers for the event. By culture the Chinese are not encouraged to be openly aggressive. However, in this case it was necessary for this group of reserved and humble students to enthusiastically seek out ways to offer the congress delegates (over 1,700) and media (over 450) every courtesy possible.

I encouraged them to be *aggressively friendly*. During the two training sessions leading up to the congress I couldn't assess whether the concept would take hold with this group. There were no questions from the group, just polite smiles. You can imagine my delight when I went to the airport to see the first group of congress delegates arrive (including my wife, daughter, and niece) when I observed no fewer than five volunteers surrounding each guest offering to carry their luggage and escort them to waiting buses and limousines. For the next few days this group of quiet, reserved students performed perhaps the best service ever rendered to a group of guests. As a matter of fact, out of the three standing ovations during the congress the volunteers got one.

Keep in mind that this vocabulary is used primarily to reinforce specific corporate values. It is an extremely powerful tool. I suggest that you examine each word you use to describe your people, your customers, your mission statement, and your values and ask yourself if they are the best possible choices.

Since leaving Disney I have become more acutely aware of other organizations that capitalize on the subtle yet all-pervasive impact language has on their employees and their customers. Language is too powerful a tool to be ignored.

Even though language is a wonderfully powerful tool for management, it is rendered useless if management's actions do not reflect it.

KEY POINTS

1. An organization's ability to create and sustain superior customer service can be tremendously enhanced through the effective use of language.

2. Proper use of language is one of the most effective ways to reinforce your corporate culture.
3. The power of language within organizations applies to any culture and any organization.
4. Language must not only be spoken, it must be practiced—especially by those in management.

It will take concerted effort from senior management to make this change. It can be done with a little hard work and diligence. Have fun doing it. You'll be pleasantly surprised by the results.

Chapter Twelve

Time

We work not only to produce but to give value to time
Eugene Delacroix
Ted Goodman, *Forbes Book of Business Quotations*

REVISITING TIME AND MOTION

As mentioned in Chapter One, at the turn of the 20th century one of the most prominent management experts was Frederick Taylor. Mr. Taylor is known as the "father of scientific management." As new manufacturing industries exploded on the American landscape, inefficiencies were rampant. With the notable exception of Henry Ford's assembly line, most businesses were simply trying to keep up with demand. Taylor and other founders and developers of scientific management revolutionized management thought and practice.

Simply stated, Taylor studied every conceivable variation in the operation of machines and workers. He proved , through his studies involving time and motions, that productivity and efficiency could be significantly improved. Early in Taylor's work at Bethlehem Steel Company (1898–1901), he asked the question, "Is there a science of shoveling?" He concluded that a man's ability to increase shoveling productivity was in part related to the weight of his shovel. Taylor gradually took on more ambitious studies and recognized a principal ingredient in scientific management. That being "intimate friendly cooperation between management and the men" (Heyel, 1973, p. 921). It is interesting that this ingredient of Taylor's research was not applied as wholeheartedly as changing the weight of shovels.

Why look back to Taylor as we look forward to the 21st century? What relevance does the "father of scientific management" have to do with the subject of creating and sustaining a superior customer service organization? The relevance is still time and motion. How do we spend our time in a service versus an industrial economy? In the 20th century and to a great degree today, much of management's time is spent focusing on maximizing productivity. This focus shows little regard for workers or for the satisfaction of customers. "Right up to the 1980's companies expected workers to 'check their brains at the door' when they arrived for work in the morning, robbing working men and women of self-respect and the cooperation of its most valuable source of knowledge and input about production processes" (Gabor, 1990, p. 42).

You have undoubtedly heard the saying that we all have the same amount of hours in a day; it's what we do with them that counts. Unfortunately, organizations waste enormous amounts of time. It is impossible to calculate the financial cost of wasting time. Wasting time is defined by all organizational activities that do not relate to serving customers.

ONE MORE TIME—IT'S THE CULTURE

It stands to reason that the more time an organization spends pleasing its customers, the happier the customers will be. Once again, the culture and structure of an organization play prominent roles. How time is spent in organizations is dictated by the organization's structure. If individualism is valued over teamwork, then managers will spend time furthering their own interests, not others'. If the organization values its workers and its customers, then managers focus on motivating their employees and pleasing their customers. It's that simple.

Managers in excellent service cultures know that their success is based on the performance of their workers. So their time and actions (motion) must be spent on taking care of their people. This is not a theory. Listen to Sam Walton, founder of Wal-Mart: "More than anything, though, I want to get across once and for all just how important Wal-Mart's associates have been to its success" (Walton, 1993, p. xii). Listen to Walt Disney, "Take care of your people, your people will take care of the customers and the money will take care of itself." Any great leader or manager will tell you the same thing. Spend your time and energy on your people!

THE CLASSIC WASTE OF TIME—STAFF MEETINGS!

Most people who have spent any amount of time in the workforce eventually find themselves attending staff meetings. The format and time for staff meetings varies greatly, some lasting for hours, others only minutes. In general most staff meetings consist of what the boss has to say. Period. In a large number of cases no action items are written down, followed up, or executed before the next meeting. Some, on the other hand, are wonderfully informative, well thought out, and smoothly run. Unfortunately, they are the exception to the rule.

In my opinion, most staff meetings are a colossal waste of time, resources, and money for one simple reason—THEY DO NOT FOCUS ON THE CUSTOMER! Typically, staff meetings mainly serve the egos of the management.

What percentage of time spent in meetings is used to discuss how the organization can better serve its customers? If you've worked in typical organizations, the percentage is negligible.

LETTING GO OF POWER

In order to ensure that meetings focus on customers, you might want to try changing your format. First, rotate the responsibility of your staff meetings to different members of the team, regardless of rank or status. Yes, you read correctly. Let everyone on the staff take turns running the staff meetings. This practice will serve to empower employees and encourage teamwork. This way everyone gets a chance to contribute. There are several benefits to this approach. Management must trust employees to perform a management function, which will boost morale. By taking an active part in the organization of the meetings, employees acquire new skills and confidence in making presentations and working in groups. By diversifying the responsibilities across the staff, politics and posturing are often reduced or eliminated. I've also found it helpful to announce who will run the next meeting as you conclude the present one. Not only will it give people time to prepare, but it will also get everyone to focus on the issues at hand—issues that are likely to resurface in the following week's agenda.

Allowing employees to conduct meetings has deeper implications for managers than just increasing employee attention and involvement. It means managers have to let go of their self-proclaimed power and give up being in control of everything. As a manager, your responsibility is to make sure that employees have the necessary resources, moral support, and encouragement to get their jobs done. For many managers, this relinquishment of power is easier said than done, because they have been trained to run things and they perceive running meetings as their right. Unfortunately, many managers believe that respect comes with authority. It doesn't. If you want power and respect, you can only get it from willing employees. Look at it another way. If an army general, with all his stars, medals, and ribbons, orders his troops to attack an enemy position, how much power would he have if they refused to do it? What could the general do all by himself? Managers, like generals, can only be as successful as the people who work with them.

Late in Walt Disney's life a small boy asked him what he did with his time every day.

"Do you draw cartoons?" the boy asked.

"No, I don't draw cartoons," Disney replied.

"Do you make movies?" the boy continued.

"No, I don't make movies," Disney said.

Frustrated, the child asked "Then what do you do?"

Disney smiled. "Son, think of me as a bumble-bee. I go around pollinating people and ideas."

Walt Disney received 48 Academy Awards, more than anyone else in history. Ask yourself how many he would have won if he tired to do all the hard work himself. Take your turn with the rest of the team.

THE ONE-HOUR MEETING

One tested and proven way to avoid long-drawn-out meetings is to keep them to one hour. Here's the catch. It is amazing how much you can get done in an hour. But if time is a concern, schedule them for either 11:00 AM or 4:00 PM—it just about guarantees they will end in an hour.

SAMPLE MEETING AGENDA

Here is what I consider to be a good agenda for a typical staff meeting:

Agenda Item	Time
Welcome and Introductions (if appropriate)	2–4 Minutes

Here is an opportunity to introduce new staff members and the meeting leader.

Exceeding Customer Expectations	30 Minutes

This is the time when you get the opportunity to focus the organization directly on the customer. The discussion should concentrate on what the staff did during the past week (or since the last meeting) to exceed customer expectations. Rather than having each person mention what they did personally, ask the staff to report on each other's accomplishments. This technique benefits the organization in two ways: it places emphasis on how much management values it employees and customers, and it provides an opportunity for people to be recognized for outstanding performance in front of their peers and management.

Organizational Support   10–15 Minutes

This time is reserved to discuss ways to support the front line. I suggest you *establish a top-ten priority list* and post it on a wall or a screen in front of the group in order to focus their attention. You should be prepared to reprioritize the list as required. Each time one of the priority items is successfully completed, celebrate it. Serve soda and popcorn if you want to, but the point is to do something out of the ordinary. Celebrating successes is a sure way of having more success.

Open Discussion   *Time Remaining*

I suggest you use this time to cover administrative information and open discussion items.

This agenda places emphasis on where it counts: serving customers through employees. If you give this approach a try, I believe you'll find that you waste less time while actually improving the morale and overall effectiveness of your staff. Allow a few weeks to get this format embedded into your meetings; it may take some time. As the manager you can jump start the process by making sure you compliment your staff's outstanding service.

We all have the same amount of time. Spend it wisely.

KEY POINTS

1. More than 90 years ago, Frederick Taylor, the "father of scientific management," advocated an "intimate friendly cooperation between management and the men." Managers in the Information Age would be wise to heed his advice.

2. Organizations waste an enormous amount of time doing things that are unrelated to satisfying their customers.

3. Organizational cultures play a significant role in determining how time is spent.

4. Staff meetings should be led by everyone on the staff. Managers should relinquish control.

5. Task lists should be prioritized and completed.

6. Regular staff meetings should be scheduled from 11 AM–noon or 4–5 PM.

7. Staff meetings should focus on how the organization can better serve its customers.

Chapter Thirteen

The Customers' Experience

Exceed your customers' expectations. If you do they will come back over and over again. —Rules for Building a Business.

Sam Walton, *Made in America*

THE GENIUS OF SAM WALTON

The late Sam Walton understood how to exceed his customers' expectations. Prior to his death, he was the wealthiest man in America. His genius was in his strong belief that his front-line employees actually ran his organization. His belief was that they—not his managers—were the ones who exceeded Wal-Mart customers' expectations. This understanding can be seen in Walton's legendary appreciative behavior toward his employees. He once promised his workers that if they reached certain financial goals he would dance the hula in Times Square. They met the goals; he danced in New York. Everybody had a good laugh, but Walton had used the "joke" to push his employees to a higher level of performance. He knew that providing a positive work environment for his people was at the core to the long-term success of his business.

The task of providing a positive working environment for employees is enhanced whenever an organization concentrates on keeping its workers motivated. The reason is simple: The customer is on the receiving end of how the employees behave. Like it or not, it is the employees' actions and attitudes toward customers that determines how well your products/services are built or how well your customers are serviced.

As a result, the importance of creating and sustaining a positive environment for your employees cannot be overstated. But customer satisfaction and loyalty are also influenced by other factors such as the physical appearance of the company as well as the systems that operate within it.

THE CUTOMERS' EXPERIENCE AND YOUR ORGANIZATION

To analyze your customers' experiences, try putting yourself into their shoes by asking the following questions: How are your customers greeted by the people they come in contact with within your organization? What does the person greeting them look like? How are they dressed? What impression are security, receptionist, groundskeeper, food service, and maintenance staffs giving your customers? Keep in mind that each contact a customer has with your organization contributes to his or her opinion of it.

If a customer or prospect receives something from you in the mail, how does it appear (attractive, correctly spelled, well composed, etc.)? What do they see when they come in physical contact with your organization? What does your lawn and lobby look like? Is the area clean? Is anything out of place? What do the signs look like? How do they read—are they friendly, hospitable, helpful? Can guests easily find who or what they are looking for? Are the leaves or plants healthy or dead? Do your colors clash? Are the seats comfortable in waiting areas? Is there any reading material in the area? Is it current and appropriate? Is there any trash in the area? How is your product or service perceived? The list is endless, but the impact of all these subtle signals is powerful. All contribute to the impression customers have of your organization.

Here is an example of a small detail that made a big impression on me. In December of 1987, I checked into a Stouffer's hotel. A neatly uniformed doorman and a number of pleasantly smiling bellman greeted me. The lobby was beautifully appointed. Everything was as I expected a Stouffer's hotel to be. What I didn't expect was what I observed in the elevator. On the floor was a carpet that read: "Have a Pleasant Thursday." The next day the message wished everyone a "Happy Friday." I thought, great touch! Someone had an idea that further enhanced the customers' experience. It just so happened that the purpose of my visit to this hotel was to give a customer service speech to several hundred people. Guess what example I used to illustrate how to enhance the customers' experience?

Everything the customer experiences must be considered a part of the total impression the customer has about the organization. If I ordered a hot breakfast the next morning and it was cold or the service was slow, these negative experiences would subtract from my overall perception of the organization. Attention to detail and consistently providing quality products and services are keys to success.

DEPARTING THE STUDIO FOR THE LIVE SHOW

It is no accident that Walt Disney World is the most popular vacation destination in the world. Everything in the park was designed with both the employees' and the customers' experiences in mind. Employees are among the friendliest, and customers are among the most loyal and satisfied, in any business.

Walt Disney was a master at designing and creating wonderful products, often going to great lengths to achieve what is referred to as the Disney "magic." Prior to opening Disneyland in California in the mid-fifties, Disney primarily produced films. With films, Walt and his team could revise every aspect of the scripts, visuals, and sound before the movie would be released to the public. But when he looked at opening a "live" show at Disneyland, he knew he would face a different type of challenge because he was dealing with human dynamics. This new variable in his product jeopardized his ability to maintain the company's growing reputation for excellence. He knew that if a guest had a negative experience he couldn't simply change it to a positive one by going back to the design studio.

Faced with the tremendous challenge of building its first theme park, the Disney teams set out to design and build an environment that would allow visitors (Guests) to be totally immersed in a special place called the "Magic Kingdom." To do this, every possible aspect of a Guest's experience was carefully considered. For example, what the Guest smelled in certain areas of the park was taken into consideration. The result is that when a Guest enters the park on Main Street USA, the aroma of fresh popcorn pervades the air. The smell of fresh popcorn fits appropriately into the aura of a turn-of-the-20th century street scene.

What the Guests hear was also factored into the design. Differently themed areas of the park such as Fantasyland, Frontierland, or Tomorrowland all have their own soundtracks playing music that reflects the mood of the lands. Unless Guests stop and deliberately listen, they cannot distinguish the point where one music theme changes to another.

SUSTAINING THE SETTING

What the Guests see at the parks was carefully considered. At Disney World in Orlando, Florida, Guests' experience starts with the highway entrance to the park areas. A six-mile entrance highway is beautifully landscaped and kept immaculately clean to create the impression of a transition between the real everyday world and that of a "Magic Kingdom." The only sign you see (at the time I was with Disney) was the one that encourages you to turn your AM radio dial to a Disney station that gives you pertinent information about the parks.

I distinctly remember the tremendous emphasis Disney management put on the cleanliness of the park. The one phrase I remember hearing the most was "One soda can on the ground could ruin the setting, thus ruining the experience of the guests." It was so true. To understand the meaning of this statement all you need to do is to try this simple exercise. Pick out any setting that is immaculately designed and kept up. It could be a beautifully appointed room, a lobby, or a freshly cut lawn in springtime. Now place a piece of rubbish, a can, or a newspaper in the middle of the setting. Guess what your eyes are drawn to? Yes, you see the garbage. This distracts greatly from the beauty of the setting, thus ruining what could be a positive impression of your organization.

THE DISNEY LOOK

A large number of Guests at Disney parks comment that Disney employees have a certain look about them. That certain look was created by Walt Disney in the early days and has continued to today. He established extremely high standards for his employees and strict stipulations regarding their appearance. Everything from hair color and cut, length of fingernails, a fresh costume daily, makeup, jewelry, restrictions on the amount of rings per hand, and size of earrings were regulated. Certain types of footwear had to be worn in compliance with company standards; cast members could not wear dark sunglasses because the Guests would not have eye contact with them. Male employees were not allowed to have facial hair. All of these restrictions were made in the name of consistency. Disney didn't want anyone or anything to look out of place and ruin the "show." Can you imagine Snow White with purple hair, dangling earrings, and dark burgundy lipstick?

Walt Disney ran into tremendous resistance for his strict dress and grooming codes—both inside as well as outside the company. The argument most heard was "dress had nothing to do with how well people did their jobs." Resistance ran particularly high during the sixties when it seemed every man wore long hair and many women dressed to express their discontentment with the establishment.

When conducting research for my Disney business seminars, I discussed the dress code issue with Dick Nunis, the then president of Walt Disney World. He made a point of stressing how much Walt insisted on the dress requirements. "Walt was so insistent, it hurt chances of recruiting some very good people during times the organization could have used them," he explained. "But he was unwavering. Walt wanted a certain look for his people and he was willing to stand up for his principles." As far as Walt Disney was concerned, having a strict dress code that created a uniform look was another way of eliminating any Guest's distractions, just like the music, the scents, and the appropriate costumes for the staff. It was another step in ensuring that the customer's experience was always positive.

While it is unlikely that your company is going to need to pipe in music, fill the lobby with artificial scents, or landscape the highway leading to your office door, you can influence a number of the elements your customers come in contact with. Whether it is the appearance of your employees, buildings, products, services, lobbies, or advertisements, each is important in shaping your customers— or prospective customers'—perception of you. It stands to reason that if customers have a more positive impression of your company than that of a competitor, you'll retain their business.

To truly understand the customers' experience of your company, one must "be a customer." You must look at your organization through the eyes of those who approach you and form impressions of your self, your employees, and the products or services you offer with every interaction. You must intentionally analyze each and every aspect of your organization that customers come in contact with—employees, advertising, buildings, products, lobbies, *everything*—and then determine how it can be enhanced.

SYSTEMS AND SMILES

While you are evaluating how to motivate employees and enhance the experience of your customers, I would be remiss not to mention including your "systems" in this process. The term "systems" refers to the day-to-day operational equipment, procedures, and practices that form the operations of your organization.

This includes everything from the machines found on the assembly line to the computers on everyone's desktops to the policies used to hire and fire employees.

If you doubt the critical importance of the role these systems play, consider the words of Carl Sewell, who is this country's top luxury-car dealer in Dallas, Texas. His commitment to service is legendary. Sewell writes in his book *Customers for Life*: "Being nice to people is just 20% of providing good customer service, the important part is designing systems that allow you to do the job right the first time. All the smiles in the world aren't going to help if our product or service is not what the customer wants" (1990, p. 24).

In 1999, candy retailers threatened law suits against the Hershey Corporation. Candy wasn't getting distributed to stores because Hershey's newly installed computer system was malfunctioning. If you're ever in doubt about the importance of systems to customer satisfaction, give the executives at Hershey a call (Nelson and Ramstad, 1999).

Not too long ago most banks had a system that allowed people to get cash from their accounts by standing in long lines waiting for a bank teller. The teller would check if the customer had enough money in his or her account and then physically count the money as he or she took it from their cash drawer, then count it again in front of the customer. That system seems archaic today because the Automated Teller Machine (ATM) has for the most part replaced the teller. Even though the ATM system effectively replaced tellers, there is still a need for financial institutions to ensure that their new systems meet customer needs. One of the most interesting occurrences resulting from business/system improvements is that customers quickly become accustomed to the improvements. Once that occurs they expect to receive the improved level of service from that point on. So those who offer continual improvements of their products and services force their competitors to either catch up or go out of business. If a bank opening today refuses to install ATM services they'd be out of business in no time.

SOLUTIONS THROUGH EMPLOYEES

Often the best and simplest way to improve systems is to ask the employees closest to them to offer suggestions. Several years ago my brother John was asked to participate in his company's "process improvement program." At the time he worked for the Norton Company, which produced a variety of manufactured products in Worcester, Massachusetts. One of the biggest problems it faced was the movement of finished products from their final assembly to the warehouse for distribution. This problem stemmed from the fact that their buildings were built incrementally over decades to match the growth and product diversification of the company. The result was that the buildings performed separate functions and caused havoc when it came time to move the finished products for distribution. My brother came up with a simple but brilliant idea: He suggested cutting holes in upper floors and lowering parts through the holes down to the bottom floor for final assembly and shipping. The idea saved millions of dollars and time for the company. Who better than John and his fellow employees to solve a problem they lived with on a daily basis?

Do not underestimate the subtle but powerful perceptions and feelings of your customers and employees. Just because you can't observe them doesn't mean they do not exist.

KEY POINTS

1. Sam Walton sincerely appreciated his front-line staff because he knew that they were the people the customers encountered.

2. The more positive customers' experiences are within organizations, the better the organization is in a competitive environment.

3. Review every physical aspect of your organization and the systems and practices that operate within it for ways to improve the customer's experiences and perceptions.

4. One way to ensure continual quality improvement of your organization is to occasionally test the environment. Pretend you are

a visitor or, better yet, have visitors critique your entire organization and report their impressions and feelings. Do not announce these visits in advance.

5. Ask your front-line employees how they'd improve their jobs as they relate to customer service. They would love to tell you.

Chapter Fourteen

Reinforcing and Changing Culture

You can employ men and hire hands to work for you,
but you must win their hearts to have them work with
you.

William J.H. Boetcker
Ted Goodman, *Forbes Book of Business Quotations*

INSTILLING DESIRED BEHAVIOR

Superior customer service organizations create and sustain their
superiority because their corporate culture is focused on meeting
or exceeding customer expectations. Throughout this book I have
stressed the importance of culture to an organization. In this chapter, I will address how organizations can instill and encourage employee behavior that results in better customer service. Conversely,
it is important to discuss ways to discourage or stop undesired behavior.

As a manager you must make the assumption that employees
are basically good, well-meaning people. They do not come to
work intent on being punished. Instead, like every other human
being (managers included) they seek acceptance, recognition, reward, and pride in their accomplishments and contributions. Any-

one reading this might question why I even mention something so obvious. Unfortunately, management has not always viewed employees in this light. The relationship between labor and management hasn't always been good, from the thousands of labor strikes in the thirties to the current movement to unionize dot-coms.

In some corporate cultures in the United States as well as overseas, there are continual reminders of labor discontent and management abuse. Any managers reading this book who are serious about creating and sustaining a superior customer service organization need to shed the view that employees are somehow different from them. We all have the same needs.

RECOGNITION

Recognizing and rewarding employees is one of the most powerful motivational tools managers have. Recognition can substantially aid in providing employees with positive experiences. The employees share that positive attitude with customers.

There are countless ways to provide recognition. It's unlikely that there will ever be a universally accepted set of methods to recognize and motivate people, because we're dealing with the complexity of human behavior. Individuals are unique and they are motivated in different ways at different times during their lives.

However, in order to create and sustain a superior customer service organization, institutionalized recognition practices need to be in place. By institutional recognition I am referring to an organization that intentionally plans to recognize its employees at certain times and after certain occurrences in the employees' careers. This recognition may be financial or otherwise.

It's also important to understand that human beings need to receive recognition throughout their work lives, not only when they first report to work or at their retirement parties. It's not enough to do thoughtful things for people when they expect it, or when the spirit moves you. You and your organization must employ meaningful recognition methods and procedures in order to continually motivate your people.

There are three basic categories of employee recognition: institutional, behavioral, and others.

Institutional recognition includes raises, benefits, vacations, sick days, and service awards, such as 5, 10, 15, and 20-year pins. These incentives are usually given at predetermined times. They are perceived as customary and expected by the employees. The fact that most employees expect them does little for their long-term motivation. In fact, if they are not received, or are late in being awarded, they can demotivate people.

Behavioral recognition focuses on the way management behaves toward employees. Management's attitude toward employees significantly affects them, both negatively and positively.

Other forms of recognition account for rewards or incentives that are not perceived as customary. For example, let's say that you give one of your employees a plane ticket to visit a hospitalized relative. The ticket is, of course, not customary, yet it is a great way to recognize and motivate your employee and won't be forgotten.

Recognition comes in many forms and successful programs must contain the right mix of incentives. However, the majority of organizations choose to give off-the-shelf awards. Plaques are a good example. They are easy to order, standardized, and ready for distribution. "The Outstanding Employee of the Month," "Manager of the Year, " "Salesman of the Quarter." Very little thought is given to the net impact on the person receiving the recognition. Perhaps a day off or bonuses would be more motivation than a standard plaque. Let's be honest, who does the plaque motivate more, the recipient or the manager giving the plaque?

Organizations must distribute the appropriate recognition at the appropriate times. If an employee will be celebrating his or her 10th anniversary at the company on January 5th, don't wait until the end of the month to congratulate him or her. Employees should feel that they're receiving recognition in a timely manner.

Finally, whatever the motivational methods, techniques, rewards, or programs implemented, management sincerity must also be present. If sincerity and gratitude aren't present, then don't expect your people to be motivated. I've seen some cases where management insincerity actually backfired. The employees resented management's attempt to patronize them.

It is helpful to think of recognition as a recipe: recognition must be applied at the *right time*, contain the *right amount of value* (not necessarily monetary), and be *given with sincerity* in order to accomplish maximum effectiveness.

The good news is that there are literally thousands of ways to reward and recognize people and they don't have to cost a lot of money. Some examples include: *special dedication areas* with employees' names, initials, birth dates, or other information. Steven Jobs, cofounder of Apple Computer, had the signatures of the 47 Macintosh Computer creators embossed on the inside of the computer's back panel.

This motivational method is perhaps best illustrated at Walt Disney World in Orlando, Florida. Walt recognized several key people who were instrumental in the planning and construction of Disney World by placing their names and associated responsibilities on the windows along Main Street USA. For example, James Passilla, Director of Casting, and for Disney's President Dick Nunis, Original Gym Supervision. What I found was most fascinating and in keeping with Walt's style of management was where his name was placed. Although well deserving, his name was not out on the street so everyone could see it. Instead, it was placed around the corner at the end of Main Street USA. It reads, "Walter Elias Disney, Graduate School of Design and Master Planning."

Take pictures: Displaying pictures of employees in prominent places continues to be a popular motivational technique. Of course, it is important that the photographs are complimentary to the employees. When the pictures are taken to celebrate awards it's important to have the employees feel that they earned the recognition. One of the more innovative employee picture programs I've seen was at Stew Leonard's grocery store in Norwalk, Connecticut. Once an employee makes "Employee of the Month," their picture is displayed near the checkout counters during that particular month. Then the employee's picture is placed with past winners' photos on a special wall in the main store area where it resides permanently. Stew Leonard, Sr., told me that former winners regularly return to his store years after they've left the company to "show off" their pictures. A master of employee recognition, Leonard's stores rank among the best in the world.

Plaques: Plaques are one of the most-often-used recognition methods. But unless they are designed with meaning they won't achieve maximum results. Here's an example: In 1992, I had the opportunity to be involved in the Summer Olympics in Barcelona for EDS. EDS was a sponsor of the Games and there were about 20 EDS employees on the marketing and hospitality team I worked with. Upon returning to the United States, I asked the in-house graphics designers to come up with a special plaque that would be treasured by the team long after the event. The design was fantastic! They incorporated unused "A" Olympic event tickets (the best tickets) that were from each person's favorite Olympic event. The tickets were framed and placed within a brightly colored background depicting the colors of the Olympic rings. The team really appreciated the thought that went into the award.

Attendance Award Program: One company I visited awarded colored stars noting attendance accomplishments. If an employee didn't miss a day in six months they would receive a blue star, a gold star after a year, and so forth. The company displayed an attendance chart with the names of all employees along with their stars, above the time card machine. It reminded me of grade school but it also kept people coming to work on time because these stars would earn employees cash awards. Everyone loved the program and most everyone came to work on or before time.

Meals with Management: Regularly scheduling breakfast or luncheon meetings with your employees, either individually or in small groups, is a great way to motivate your people. It also gives the executives an opportunity to get closer to front-line activities. It's not a good idea to invite a supervisor to come along with his or her front-line staff since this can inhibit conversation. Meet them separately.

First-Name Badges: When I first received my name badge at the new employee orientation at Disney I didn't comprehend its significance. But just like my first new-recruit haircut in the military it symbolized membership into a special organization. Having my badge meant that I was an official member of the Disney organization. Keep in mind that I wasn't a kid at the time; I was a fairly well-seasoned executive. Yet I had a youthful feeling of pride. I wasn't alone. Nearly everyone appeared to have the same feeling. A long-time Disney manager told me that he thought the first-name badge was the single most important motivational tool the organization had. This was true because it broke down barriers between ranks. By having no visible identification outside of a name badge, employees are allowed to easily communicate with each other, regardless of rank. I called the president Dick versus Mr. Nunis. I can't tell you how good it felt to call people by their first names. By the way, if you are like most people and have a tough enough time remembering names, the first-name badge is a wonderful aide. Just make the letters large enough so you can read them from a distance. Remember, if you want to get the most out of the badges, everyone in the organization must wear them at all times during working hours.

Employee-Customer Meetings: Why not have your best employees rewarded by meeting your customers? Give them a chance to see how their labors fit into the overall scheme of things. In most cases it only takes a few minutes. I'm positive, the vast amount of customers would enjoy the meetings as well.

While on the subject of customers, I must caution you to never, ever ignore your employees when you have special guests or customers in your workplace. In addition to being inconsiderate, the employees get a clear message as to how valuable you really think they are. Figure out a way to at least acknowledge them. I see this demotivator happening too frequently. It delivers a silent, negative impact to your employees' self-esteem. You wouldn't bypass the president's office with a special guest without a good reason. I recommend you do the same for your employees.

Managers/Executives, Front-Line Jobs: Some organizations successfully sponsor periods of time when managers/executives work the front-line jobs of their organizations. This practice not only can provide motivation for employees, but it also gives managers an appreciation for what the "troops" go through on a day-to-day basis.

SAYING THANKS IN ADVANCE

One employee motivational technique that Disney management used was to recognize people while they were training to perform a large job. When the EPCOT Center was about to have its 15th anniversary, the Disney marketing department wanted to draw attention to this fact by conducting one of the biggest press events in its history. The entire cast (including me) had to lend a hand. Some used their own cars to pick up media representatives at local hotels, while others worked in the parks instead of their offices. It was a big deal and everyone was required to attend meetings, briefings, and special training sessions to meet the challenge. What struck me was not the immense amount of resources required to pull the event off, but the fact that nearly every time I turned around I was being thanked and given things like T-shirts, hats, and free lunches—all before the actual event occurred. In other words, the employees were being thanked in anticipation of the great job they had not yet done. This practice nearly guaranteed that the job would be extremely well done. So instead of waiting to see how hard people worked and then showing appreciation, they were thanked before they performed the job. More than just a great idea, it was one that worked.

There are many more great ways to recognize employees. You may want to ask your employees what they would really appreciate. I remember asking one of my administrative assistants that question during Secretary's Week. I must admit that I thought she would say something like flowers or candy. Instead, she asked if she could have an afternoon off because her daughter was coming home from college and she wanted to surprise her. I still got her a small gift, and I know she enjoyed the afternoon off. It's often the little things that go a long way.

DISCIPLINING EMPLOYEES

If you do everything in your power to create an environment so your people will be happy, you might then feel that there wouldn't be a need to discipline them. Unfortunately, being human, employees will inevitably have marital problems, health problems, in-law problems, child problems, and financial problems, and they will drag all or part of them to work. Some, by their very nature, will create situations that require discipline. I hope you won't encounter these folks too often. At best, you can influence people at work by creating a positive environment and hope that it will extend into their personal lives. But how do you balance a workplace wrought with factors you can't control? Quite honestly, there are no easy answers, only guidelines.

The purpose of rewarding people is to recognize them for a particular deed or accomplishment, and that reward can motivate them to continue that type of behavior. It's often assumed that the opposite is true for discipline or punishment. When punishment occurs the obvious goal is to discourage the offender from committing the offense again.

Unfortunately, rewards, as well as punishment, don't always produce expected results. This fact exists everywhere in society, including the workplace where people know what is expected of them. They know if they come in late several time without good reason, or if they steal from the organization, they will be punished. Assuming that people unknowingly violate procedures and policies, it is incumbent upon management to first ask themselves the question: "What could I have done that would have prevented the employee from making a particular error or committing a violation?"

I cannot overemphasize the importance of this point. Be honest! What could have been done prior to employees making mistakes or committing violations of company rules to prevent the infraction? Had the organization taken the time to communicate its desires and followed up to ensure that the communication was understood? By making sure people thoroughly understood expectations, many problems would be avoided. It isn't so much what we communicate, but how we express ourselves that counts. Do we communicate as a matter of necessity to cover ourselves, or do we communicate because we care that our employees avoid the embarrassment of making mistakes? Most of the time, we find that employees don't mean to commit offenses. After all, people do not come to work intending to make mistakes. They want to be successful and to be recognized accordingly.

Many times managers blame the "dumb" employee in an effort to distance themselves from taking responsibility for problems. They want to avoid being punished themselves. But this type of action does not get at the root of the problem, and more than likely the offense or mistake will reoccur. In cases like this, those in management who are quick to blame will never contribute to building or sustaining a superior organization.

I think it's fair to say that some of our most valuable lessons in life have been learned through our mistakes, but we don't necessarily need to receive punishment or be embarrassed to learn our lessons. In fact, in most cases when we know we unintentionally goofed, and we know that our superior also knows and has chosen not to negatively comment, we learn two things: to appreciate our manager for not criticizing us, and to learn from our mistake. Just as there are countless ways to reward people, there are countless ways to punish them. They range from an unfriendly glare or comment from a manager to termination.

Executive behavior is a good example. Without realizing it, executives can send messages out to the workforce with debilitating, punishing results. I recall one incident where the CEO of a large company commented that one day he was simply having a bad day. He wasn't mad at anyone. Ordinarily, he was very friendly. On this particular day, he passed a group of employees without greeting them. He just kept his head down and walked by. The next thing he knew, a rumor was circulating throughout the company that the company was in some sort of trouble. He was shocked to realize that he had that kind of influence on the organization. Here is a case where a form of punishment (fear/uncertainty) was caused inadvertently.

It's also fair to say that punishment can leave emotional scars that are sometimes impossible to heal. Several years ago, I was asked by a corporate executive of a large company in the Northeast to consult on a few problems in his sales division. Sales were down and a number of good, young salespeople were leaving the company. I began my work by endeavoring to understand the sales process. To accomplish this I took a look at how sales opportunities were supported or rejected by internal management. Only by understanding this process could I know where the problems were.

I didn't have to go far to get a good feel for the problem. Each Monday morning, salespeople would have their sales opportunities (deals) reviewed by a group of senior executives. I was told that the purpose of these meetings was to offer guidance and support to the salespeople. It was a semiformal process, which included having the executives asking probing, sometimes difficult questions of the salespeople.

The meeting room was dimly lit to allow visual presentations to be more easily read. To me, the room looked like a dungeon. The salespeople had to wait their turn outside in a hallway. I observed each salesperson trying to "adjust" their eyes to the darkness as they initially fumbled through their slide presentations. The outcome of these meetings meant everything to the salespeople. Their sales opportunities that they worked so hard on were funded, rejected, or delayed as a result of these meetings. The pressure on them was great. At the executive table I noticed a kind of "friendly combat" going on between subgroups of executives. They appeared to be competing against each other, rather than focusing their attention on guiding the salespeople; they would go off on meaningless tangents. To the executives, this was a time to show how smart they were in front of their peers. To the young salespeople, however, it was a time of great apprehension, unrest, and sometimes downright fear.

In one particular meeting I attended, a young man appeared before the executives with a sales opportunity he had obviously worked long and hard on. He explained in great detail why the company should give him more funding to pursue his sale. Instead of receiving support from the group, they attacked the sales opportunity from every side. They argued among themselves for at least 20 minutes. The salesman appeared to be taking the criticism in stride, but it was obvious to me that he was taking the whole thing personally. I sensed he felt his professional pride, not to mention his career, was being damaged forever.

After the meeting, I went to the salesman's office to see how he was doing. I knew he had to be hurting inside. Like the "young trooper" he was, he felt he was supposed to act tough, he told me he was fine and that the meeting didn't bother him as much as it apparently bothered me. I knew he was hiding his true feelings, but I decided not to continue to dwell on the subject. A month or so after this incident the young man quit the company. He got a job with one of the company's chief competitors. It didn't surprise me. I decided to call him to ask why he quit, just to see if he would be honest with me. I also needed to know why because of the consulting work I was doing. His exact words to me cannot be repeated but he did make a promise I suspect he will keep. His promise was that each time he competed against his old employer he would work especially hard to beat them. He felt disdain for his former company and everything it stood for.

In the meantime, each Monday morning the executives got their chance to show off their great intelligence to each other. Here was a form of *institutional punishment*.

You may have the impression that I'm recommending you go light on people when it comes to punishment. For the most part you are correct. However there are times when you must act swiftly and decisively. There are times when people cross into what I call the "danger zone." Once they enter into this zone you must not hesitate to act. There are two broad categories where this applies:

1. When flagrant violations occur, such as theft, or intentional endangering of people or property. The Disney organization did not hesitate in dismissing a cast member who endangered people. Fighting among employees was not tolerated; never mind striking a guest.

2. The second category relates to violations that cause the loss of business. This is where an employee of the organization, in no mat-

ter what position, commits an offense against the organization or customers that directly impacts the business. For example, let's say an employee insults a customer. In some organizations "standing up to the customer" is encouraged. I could never understand this mentality. In excellent customer service organizations, I've observed this offense being punishable by immediate dismissal. I distinctly remember that at Disney using profane language in front of a Guest was punishable by immediate dismissal, end of discussion. There are exceptions of course, but as a rule this type of behavior is not tolerated by anyone.

You must establish your "danger zones" with your employees very early in their employment stage. They must know clearly and in no uncertain terms what behavior will be tolerated and what behavior will be punished and to what degree. Punishment must be distributed fairly. If you make exceptions you will seriously hurt your organization's ability to regulate good and bad behavior. Thus, you inject a sense of unfair play into the corporate culture.

KEY POINTS

Recognizing Employees

1. Employee recognition is one of the most powerful tools a manager has to motivate employees.
2. There are no universally accepted ways to motivate all employees all the time.
3. Successful employee recognition programs are institutionalized. This means that at certain points in time during their careers employees receive recognition.
4. Basically, there are three categories into which employee recognition falls: institutional, behavioral, and other.
5. Management's attitude toward employees and their subsequent recognition are critical to employee motivation.
6. Recognition must be given at the right time, in the right amount, and with sincerity in order to yield maximum benefit.

Disciplining Employees

1. In most, if not all, cases that are likely to require discipline, make sure you look at yourself to determine if you or the organization contributed to the problem. Look hard. It may very well be that you could help solve the problem by changing something within the organization.

2. Make sure you have all the facts before you act. I learned a long time ago that most decisions I made in haste created larger problems than the original one I tried to solve.

3. Don't judge people. Everyone, including you and me, needs to be given the benefit of the doubt once in a while.

4. Distribute punishment fairly. Your people, peers, and superiors will form their opinions about you from your actions. You want to be perceived as fair.

5. When you criticize it is often helpful to the person receiving the criticism to hear you say that either you committed a similar mistake or you knew of an important person who made a similar mistake. In some cases this technique allows you to focus in on the problem rather than focusing on the employee.

6. Try to solve the problem with the employee. Monitor the problem to see that it doesn't reoccur.

7. Make it clear to your people what is tolerated within your organization and what is not. There are sacred cows in each organization (e.g., no alcoholic beverages consumed during business hours, no foul language, dress codes, etc.). I suggest, however, that you take a look at why you have such rules. Do they have a direct impact on what your customers think about your organization? This is the area where the most emphasis should be put regarding reward and punishment. The closer the action comes to the customer, the more intense the reward and punishment.

Chapter Fifteen

Applying the Principles

Most of us at one time or another have been part of a "great team," a group of people who functioned together in an extraordinary way—who trusted one another, who complemented each other's strengths, goals, and who produced extraordinary results . . . Many say that they have spent much of their lives looking for that experience again.

Peter M. Senge, *The Fifth Discipline*

THE INFORMATION TECHNOLOGY PAVILION

I will always regard my time at Disney as a pivotal period in my life, one in which I began to learn the "secrets" of superior customer service organizations. Once I thought I had acquired a fairly definitive understanding of how Disney achieved superior service, I decided to take the next step. In essence, I could no longer be content just to understand how to create and run superior customer service organizations, I felt that the only way to validate what I had learned was to leave Disney and apply my newfound knowledge within another corporate culture. The challenge was to see if I could, in fact, integrate a service excellence culture into a corporation that didn't have the benefit of Walt Disney as its founder, one that didn't aspire to deliver happiness as a product.

My opportunity came in 1988 with EDS. EDS is a world leader in the business of providing information technology services. It's important to know that I had very little knowledge of the information technology industry, because what you are about to read is living proof that the management premises contained in this book really work.

ACCEPTING A CHALLENGE

After spending a few years working within the EDS government division, I was asked to move to Dallas, Texas, to head up a special project. Due to my association with Disney, senior management at EDS thought that I was the candidate to lead the creation, construction, and operation of the first public marketing center for EDS—even though I didn't posses any large-scale design or construction project experience that qualified me for the assignment. I also did not have any knowledge of EDS headquarters, resources, and department relationships that I would have to depend on for assistance on the project.

The first EDS executive that I brought on to the team as the assistant director was Ms. Bonnie Arvin. Bonnie was outstanding! She brought the knowledge of the company and the area that I had to have. Her smile, hard work, and enthusiasm throughout the project were invaluable.

EDS leased a 23,000-square-foot space in the Infomart building, which was constructed to attract technology-based companies. Located near downtown Dallas, this huge (1 million-square-foot) glass-enclosed structure housed more than 100 information technology-marketing showrooms. The Infomart is home to marketing facilities for companies such as IBM, Xerox, NCR, and AT&T and attracts more than 300,000 visitors each year.

My challenge was to develop a visual representation of EDS as the world leader in the information technology business by taking a very large space heavily populated with large steel support beams and design a marketing center that demonstrated an understanding of the entire EDS business operation worldwide.

> To create the future, a company must first be capable of imagining it. To create the future a company must first develop a powerful visual representation of what the future could be. To borrow from Walt Disney, what is required is "Imagineering." Disney imagined an experimental city of tomorrow where previously a run-down horse ranch had existed. That dream became EPCOT—part of the world's number-one tourist destination. Interestingly, EDS, another foresight- ful company hired Disney alumni (me) to help put together an exhibit demonstrating how the information technology revolution will change the way we live and work in the next century. (Hamel and Prahalad, 1994, p. 89)

DEFINING THE MISSION

Although I had no similar project experience, what I did have was an understanding of how superior organizations were created. I knew that the first step in the process was to establish a mission for the marketing center. The mission had to be simple. It would have to be repeatable by the center's employees, and understood by the customers. The visitors would determine if the mission was being fulfilled. The mission was "To build the finest marketing center of its type in the world."

FOCUS ON CUSTOMERS AND EMPLOYEES

Once the mission was established, two key principles were used to guide the project from start to finish. The first was to imagine how the guests/customers would evaluate the finished product. In order to accomplish this, everyone who worked on the project had to feel they were the guests and to visualize how the guests would feel about the Pavilion. Nearly every decision, from the creation and construction of the facility to the everyday operations, was made "through the eyes of the guest." This approach kept the focus on the customer while also providing the team with clear criteria for making decisions.

The design of the facility had to serve the needs of several important groups, including:

1. Senior executives from industry and government from around the world.
2. All forms of media, print, radio and television.
3. Technical experts. In that EDS was in the business of selling technical solutions, the center had to reflect leading-edge technologies.
4. Individuals from around the world who knew very little about, information technology.
5. Community groups; school groups; walk-in traffic; and EDS employees, their families, and friends.

The marketing center had to represent the current EDS customer base without showing favoritism to one industry or government. The center had to be easily adaptable to change as technology and marketing messages evolved. It had to be done right the first time. The center also had to accommodate administrative offices, meeting rooms, and service areas for food service and delivery, restrooms, and behind-the-scenes mechanics.

My goal was to incorporate the highest levels of quality, workmanship, materials, and technologies in order to fulfill the mission. Quite simply, we had to give all of the audiences an experience that would provide them with an understanding of the EDS scope, breadth, and capabilities worldwide.

The second principle was to demonstrate care and respect for the Pavilion employees who would represent EDS by delivering the final product/service to the center's visitors.

In addition to behaving in a supportive and appreciative manner to each of the center's employees, I went to great lengths to provide pleasant office and working space for the team at the Pavilion. I knew that eventually the employees would bring their friends and family to the center. I wanted to make sure that when they did they would feel that they "owned" it. I wanted them to feel that they were being given the respect that an owner would get. To this end, I insisted that all administrative offices have equal space regardless of anyone's title—a radical concept for any large company. But, by having equal-sized offices, I felt I could eliminate the hierarchy effect and build a sense of teamwork. All of the offices were furnished the same, the carpet was the same, and the amenities were equal. The result was a unified team of employees who were focused on a vision, proud of their working environment, not bogged down by a sense of inequality or rank.

YES! WE WOULD BUILD A STREET INDOORS

In retrospect, accepting the challenge was the easy part. Once the mission was stated and I committed to focusing on customers' and employees' experiences, the project was ready to get started. The next step was to come up with a design for the facility that could meet all of the requirements. Less than a month after accepting the challenge and gathering requirements, a design idea came to me in the middle of the night—3:01 AM on February 23, 1990, to be exact. A "street scene." Yes! We would build a street scene, where visitors could leisurely wander through "shops" that demonstrated how information technology was being applied by EDS. There would be manufacturing, government, health care, insurance, financial, transportation, and energy "stores" in the marketplace. Jumping ahead of the story, the street turned out to look so realistic that two months after it was built I had to stop a custodian from hosing the street down. The center was on the second floor of the Infomart building.

SUPPORT FROM THE TOP

Some of the EDS senior managers disagreed with the design idea—they had a valid reason. The company had grown to a multi-billion-dollar company without investing millions of dollars in a marketing showroom. To them the center was a waste of money. However, EDS Chairman Les Alberthal thought differently.

He was committed to the project. Support from the top of the organization was central to the success of the project, as it is for almost
everything in the organization. Over the next several months, a
number of the dissenting senior executives made it very clear to me
how they felt. I was at times tempted to share my concerns over their
criticisms of the project with my team. However, as the leader it was
my responsibility to shield my employees from anything that would
detract from their mission. Burdening your staff with things they
can't do anything except worry about is counterproductive.

COMMUNICATE, THEN COMMUNICATE AGAIN

I had learned from my days with Disney that I had to continually
communicate as much as I could with my team. I knew that if each
individual could "see" and "feel" the mission as strongly as I did,
then we could overcome what looked to be an impossible challenge.

As the project grew in complexity and the team grew larger, the
need for effective communications became more crucial. At times,
more than 200 EDS personnel and subcontractors were involved, and
it was critical that everyone be on the same page. I had to devise a
communication system that would reach everyone at the right time
with the right messages. I chose to have weekly meetings with everyone involved as the main medium for communication. At these
weekly meetings, everyone was invited who was involved in the project. The meetings were not confined to select groups, such as the design firm, the building contractor, or the EDS marketing and sales
teams whose "buildings" were to tell the EDS story. Everyone was invited, from the janitorial company, to the caterer, to the carpenter and
electrician—anyone who wanted to talk, share their ideas, ask questions, or needed to see how their piece of the project would fit with
someone else's. These meetings were focused on working together,
on using the power of everyone's talents and skills in harmony to
bring together the world's best marketing center.

In addition these meetings allowed for another opportunity to re-
peat the vision and mission of the Pavilion. I wanted the team to feel
mutual ownership of the project. I wanted them to define the

timelines, milestones, and deliverables in these meetings, to think through the thousands of details and decisions. I knew that this would create pride, ownership, and ultimately the quality and standards of excellence needed for the Pavilion to fulfill its mission.

Once the mission was stated and the vision for the center was accepted, the next step was to turn the design idea into reality. I insisted on working only with vendors and contractors who had the same principles of quality and customer service EDS had embedded within its corporate culture. I wanted to know how involved and committed the president and senior executives of the corporation were and how willing they were to help build the finest information technology (IT) marketing center in the world. Did they have a great track record of delivering quality on time and within budget? Finally I wanted to ensure that the internal EDS division personnel in real estate and purchasing were positive about their working relationship with the subcontractors.

DESIGN FOR THE CUSTOMER

Throughout the project, I utilized a "walk-through" approach, putting everyone involved in the project in the customers' "shoes." We were sensitive to things such as sound, lighting, colors, width of corridors, wheelchair access, and countless other items until we were completely satisfied that both the concept and space worked for the customers. One rule throughout the entire project was that nothing should seem out of place. As I learned at Disney, one thing out of place ruins the setting and if the setting was ruined, the guests will be distracted from whatever message or image you are trying to portray. These initial "walk-throughs" paid off in drastically reducing mistakes or changes.

NURTURER OF CHAMPIONS

Throughout the project, a critical role that I had to play as the leader was to be enthusiastic and encouraging versus authoritative to the team. No matter what happened, I had to stay positive, empathetic, and supportive to the team. To use the words of Tom Peters, coauthor of a classic book on management, *In Search of Excellence*, "In the excellent companies we found managers acting as nurturers of champions" (Peters and Waterman film interview, n.d.).

This nurturing approach to managing people allowed me to avoid hierarchical organizational structure. The result was an environment where everyone was involved. They were listened to, communicated with, and respected.

TRAINING THE PAVILION TEAM

As the project moved toward completion, I began to focus on the critical job of training the staff. Employees are the first people with whom Pavilion visitors would come into contact, so they had to be well trained. For this to happen, I had to take special care in all aspects of their selection, training, communication and supervision.

I decided to have the front line at the Pavilion rotate every six to eight months from the different EDS business units. They were to be called "ambassadors." Each new group of ambassadors brought with it tremendous energy and enthusiasm. The selection criteria for the ambassadors were stringent. I knew that many of our guests would form their initial impressions of EDS from their contact with this group. Each ambassador had to have a minimum of five years with EDS and go through five to six weeks of on-the-job training at the Pavilion. This training consisted of reviewing the mission and design concept of the pavilion in great detail. It also included information about EDS services and customers.

To continually focus the team on our mission, each week in our team meetings we would ask ourselves two questions. First, how did we exceed a guest's expectations? Second, how did we make the facility better? My contention was that if the team knew that each week these two questions would be asked, they would be mindful of them all week.

RECOGNIZING THE TEAM

The Pavilion took 13 months to build. A few weeks after the Pavilion opening, EDS management wanted to formally recognize each and every member of the IT Pavilion team. I felt it was critical that everyone get the credit they so richly deserved. A great deal of time and care went into the evening event, which was set in the lobby of the Infomart. Each team member was invited to bring a spouse or guest and each team member, subcontractor, and EDS business unit was recognized for his or her contributions. Each team member received a plaque signed by both EDS Chairman Les Alberthal and myself—an effort that took at least eight hours because every plaque had personal comments on them to every individual. The evening and the Pavilion were great successes. In fact, as part of our improvement processes, we surveyed our guests that first year. We achieved an "excellent/good" rating 97 percent of the time. Concurrently, that same year, we surveyed the EDS sales team. Of the EDS salespeople who brought guests to the Pavilion, more than 65 percent of these salespeople ended up in the EDS prestigious Inner Circle, which recognizes top-selling performers.

To this day the Pavilion remains a highlight in my professional career. It was the first time that I was able to apply the principles I had learned at Disney from inception to completion. As far as I know, the Information Technology Pavilion holds the record for being the most visited marketing center of its type in the world. Sandie Mayfield, one of the senior project managers, summed it up this way. "So, what did we create? A hallmark to EDS vision, teamwork, and excellence. A hallmark to true customer services." One of the guests who toured the Pavilion during the grand opening was Stanley Marcus of the famous Neiman Marcus stores. When asked his impression of the facility, he said "This Pavilion is among the finest quality I have ever seen." This stuff works!

ON TO THE OLYMPICS, WORLD CONGRESSES, AND GLOBAL SUMMITS

After the success of the Pavilion, I couldn't imagine anything that could give me more conviction that I had really understood the "secrets" to superior customer service organizations. Little did I know that the Pavilion was simply a dry run for what was about to happen.

Thirty days after the grand opening of the Pavilion, Les Alberthal offered me another challenge at EDS. This time it was to head up the EDS marketing of the 1992 Barcelona Olympics. EDS had been awarded the "Results System" at Barcelona. This meant that a team of more than 150 EDS engineers needed to prepare and operate the immensely complex task of integrating all of the electronics necessary to collect and calculate all of the event scores and provide them quickly and accurately to allow for worldwide broadcasting. Unlike the Pavilion, the product (the Olympics) was already created. While another EDS team concentrated on building the Results System, my challenge was to create a program using the Olympics as a venue to market EDS. Once again, I needed to pull together a team with a common vision and mission. Our mission for the Olympics was to "provide the finest event marketing experience in EDS history." The EDS team executed not only the marketing but also the immensely complex technical requirements that drove the Results System for the entire Olympics.

This particular assignment required planning for more than 300 EDS customers and prospective customers to attend the Olympic events. What our team had to plan for was local transportation, Olympic events (over 30), dinners, gifts, and festivities in Barcelona. EDS had a world-class Executive Briefing staff to assist on the project. They made my job easy. Our challenge was to put ourselves in the place of the guests from the time they received their invitations at home to arriving at the Olympics to the time they left Barcelona.

The Olympics were spectacular! The EDS team did a magnificent job! As I reflect back on the event the one thing that I will remember most, as I am sure the guests still remember, was how the EDS event staff people treated them. Our guests could not say enough about how they were treated. By the way, two years after the Olympics concluded, one of the arrows used in lighting the Olympic Torch in Barcelona arrived at my home. That is another story.

Based on EDS success in Barcelona, World Cup Soccer Officials approached me and asked it EDS would do the Results System when the World Cup was held in the United States in 1994. Shortly thereafter, Turner Broadcasting executives approached me and asked if EDS would be willing to consult for the Goodwill Games in St. Petersburg, Russia. EDS agreed to do both, with outstanding results. You have heard it said that success breeds success. I say that success is bred from focusing your organization around your customer and caring about the people who serve the customers.

I didn't realize at the time how valuable this large international event experience would be to my future. In 1997 the Information Technology Association of America (ITAA) won the right on behalf of the United States to host the 1998 World Congress on Information Technology. I was appointed President/CEO.

My involvement in the Olympics, the World Cup, and the Goodwill games was mainly related to marketing. However, in the World Congress I had responsibility to do everything from fundraising, creating the program, selecting the speakers, marketing the event, to filling the seats, all 1,900 of them. The World Congress would offer new and diverse management challenges. Once again, my understanding the "secrets to superior customer service organizations" would be applied.

The Olympics, World Cup, and Goodwill Games had brand names and set venues. I did not have to worry about the funding for them. For the World Congress, however, there was $200,000 seed money and the rest (over $6 million) had to be raised. All the while the planning had to occur simultaneously. I hadn't had this type of large-scale international event planning experience, but I knew how to apply the management principles of superior organizations.

The World Congress on Information Technology took place in June 1998 at George Mason University in Fairfax, Virgina. By all measures it had been the most successful in the history of the event. President Bill Clinton sent a videotaped message (he was traveling to China), Vice President Al Gore transmitted live from the White House to the congress, and Mikhail Gorbachev and Margaret Thatcher graced the stage. Steve Forbes (*Forbes Magazine*),

Michael Dell (Dell Computer), Al Berkeley (Vice Chairman Nasdaq), and government leaders from the United States, China, Taiwan, Malaysia, Korea, Japan, and Africa spoke on the program.

Nearly 200 media organizations covered the event. A record 109 corporate and government entities sponsored the event. More than 1,900 senior-level executives and government officials from 93 countries attended. If that wasn't enough of a confirmation that I was on the right track, we wrapped up our success with an excess of funds of $1,000,000 that was donated to charity. I'm sharing these examples of success—the Pavilion, The Olympics, World Cup, and World Congress and Global Summit—not to draw attention to myself, for I was just one of many individuals working on these projects, but to show you that the principles of creating and sustaining superior customer service organizations truly work. Putting the principles into action takes vision, dedication, and perseverance, but most of all it requires the dedication and loyalty of the staff. Follow the principles, and use some common sense, and you'll find the professional and personal results astounding!

POLITICAL SUPPORT

Large, international events on the scale of the World Congress must have political support from all levels of government to be truly successful. The same principles of management contained in this book were applied to working with government as well as industry. As previously mentioned, superior customer service organizations require support from the top. The World Congress was no different. However, in the case of the World Congress the top meant senior political leadership from local, state, and federal levels.

There are a number of senior political leaders and influencers who have contributed immensely to the support and success of the World Congresses on Information Technology, the Global Internet Summits, and ongoing large-scale projects with which I am involved. Katherine Hanley, Chairman of the Fairfax County (VA) Board of Supervisors and other members of the board approved funding for the seed money to bid for support for the Congress. The event would not have occurred without this funding.

Special appreciation goes to the former Governor, now Senator George Allen (1998 World Congress) and to Jim Gilmore, the present Governor of the Commonwealth of Virginia and the citizens of the Commonwealth of Virginia. Governor Gilmore is a national leader and champion of the Information Technology industry and a significant participant in the major events that I have been involved with in Virginia, Washington, and Taiwan. Governor Gilmore served as the Co-Chairman of both the 2000 and 2001 Summits. Don Upson, the Virginia Secretary of Technology, provided continual support of the World Congresses and the host of other activities that I have been and continue to be involved in. Thanks also to Caroline Boyd, Josh Leif, and Barry Du Val, the Virginia Secretary of Commerce.

The First Lady of Virginia, Roxanne Gilmore, encouraged me to become involved in what could be one of the largest events in United States history—Jamestown 2007. The year 2007 marks the 400th anniversary of the founding of our United States republic.

Special acknowledgment goes to Congressman Tom Davis (VA), Senator George Allen (VA), Senator John Warner (VA), and Congressman Jim Moran (VA) for their personal involvement and support of the 1998 World Congress and the 2000–2001 Global Internet Summits. Led by Congressman Davis, these individuals (along with other senior congressional leaders) conducted congressional briefings on the floor of the House of Representatives and Senate gallery for Global Internet Summit delegates in 2000 and 2001. It is very rare for anyone other than those in political office to sit in the seats of the House of Representatives. This illustrates the level of their support.

I would like to acknowledge the Steering Committees of the 2000–2001 Global Internet Summits and the Executive Committees of the 1998 and 2000 World Congresses. These entities are fantastic examples of superior customer focused organizations.

TAIWAN: APPLYING THE PRINCIPLES GLOBALLY

After the 1998 World Congress I left EDS after 10 years and began my own firm, Poisant International, LLC. I had the good fortune of serving as the International Executive Director for the 2000 World Congress on Information Technology in Taipei, Taiwan. This event was yet another clear example to me that not only could the "secrets" of superior customer service organizations be applied in the United States, they could be applied within an entirely different culture. A phenomenal example of an excellent customer service organization occurred at this 2000 Congress. In my opinion, this Congress surpassed the 1998 World Congress. Nearly 400 media representatives covered the event; the event sold out weeks in advance; the program was world-class. Speakers included President Shui-Bien Shen of Taiwan, Bill Gates (Microsoft), John Chambers (Cisco), Carly Fiorina (HP), Nobel Laureate Dr. Robert Mundell, Senator John D. Rockefeller, IV, Dr. William Magee, Founder, Operation Smile, and Dr. Othamn Yeop Addullah, Chairman and CEO, Multimedia Development Corporation, Malaysia.

The leadership of the Chairman of the Steering Committee, Vice Minister, Ministry of Economic Affairs, Chii-Ming Yiin, provided guidance, wisdom and full national government support. Matthew F.C. Miau, Chairman MiTac-Synnex, General (Ret.) Yun Kuo, Vice Chairman, MiTac-Synnex, and the other members of the Steering Committee worked diligently to ensure the success of the event.

The 2000 World Congress Chairman was Richard Yin, the EDS Taiwan country leader. Richard performed brilliantly through the complex maze of difficult decisions necessary to successfully execute this magnificently successful Congress. Richard's vision (mission) of hosting a truly world-class event never wavered.

On most projects, there is always one person who has the responsibility to track and implement thousands of inherent details. That person at the 2000 World Congress was its Executive Director, Arthur Hwa. Arthur dedicated every waking moment of three years to ensuring that every one of the thousands of details were followed and implemented.

Mr. James Wong, Chairman of the Information Services Industry Association of China, Taipei (CISA), led Taiwan's industry involvement throughout the years of preparation. It was CISA, under James' enthusiastic leadership, that received the award to host the 2000 World Congress on Information Technology. It was James who set the tone of excitement inside and outside his association. As in the other large events there were hundreds of others in Taiwan who worked so very hard on making the Congress a premier event for their country—I would like to acknowledge all of them. In that acknowledgment, I am confident that all of the delegates to Taiwan from around the globe fondly remember the way they were treated by the front-line employees over all other aspects of the event. There were three standing ovations during the event. One of them was for the front-line employees.

Chapter Sixteen

Managing in the "Information Age"

The digital economy requires a new kind of businessper-
son: one who has the curiosity and confidence to let go of
the old mental models and old paradigms; the tempers,
the needs for business growth and profit with the requirements of employees, customers, and society for privacy,
fairness, and a share in the wealth they create; one who
has the vision to think socially, the courage to act, and the
strength to lead in the face of coolness or even ridicule.
The digital Economy requires yesterday's managers to become tomorrow's leaders.

Don Tapscott, *The Digital Economy*

THE "INFORMATION AGE" AND GLOBALIZATION

The" Information Age" is affecting nearly every aspect of human
activity. Rapid technological advances in information technology
such as the World Wide Web (Internet) and the computer chip are
the primary drivers behind this new age. Those fortunate enough
to live in economically developed or developing countries are receiving the lion's share of the benefits derived from the Information Age. The reality around all the hype about the promises of this

new age is the vast majority of the world's population were not connected as the 21st century began.

Organizations are undergoing a metamorphosis as the Information Age takes hold. Businesses, industries, and governments are being transformed from an industrial-based to a knowledge-based economy. World markets are melding into a single marketplace becoming globalized. In Thomas Friedman's best-selling book *The Lexus and the Olive Tree* (1999), he describes globalization as the "integration of capital, technology, and information across national borders, in a way that is creating a single global market and to some degree, a global village" (inside front cover). Friedman also writes that globalization is redefining how a country measures its power and influence. "While defining measurement of the Cold War was weight—particularly the throw weight of missiles—the defining measurement of the globalization system is speed—speed to commerce, travel, communication and innovation" (p. 9).

The Information Age poses several challenges for managers. With all the changes there is one thing that never changes: *human nature*. Throughout this book I hope I have presented a compelling case for managers to recognize the importance of their people to the success of their organizations. No matter what time period or age—Industrial, Information, or Space Age—human nature does not change. The basic needs of human beings have not and will not change. Managers who understand how to meet human needs will succeed where others will continue to fail.

Michael Dertouzos, the director of the MIT Laboratory for Computer Science, wrote a best-selling book in 1997, *What Will Be: How the New World of Information Will Change Our Lives*. Perhaps what will be is what already is. Dertouzos described a world where new technologies will widen the gap between rich and poor people if left to their own devices. A world where employees at every entry level will have more decision-making power but will have to work smarter—and harder—to keep their jobs, and a world of automation and group work. Dertouzos points out that human nature has not changed from our days in caves. "Yet we carry the features and mannerisms of our ancestors as well as our common reflexes and human patterns acquired through evolution. The fear, love, anger, greed and sadness that we feel today are rooted in the caves that we inhabited thousands of years ago" (p. 300).

The fact is that businesses and organizations will continue to be affected by technology. The message is to accept change as inevitable and accept everyone as human beings.

WHAT WE THINK WE KNOW

It would be folly for anyone to predict how the Information Age will end up impacting managers, businesses, organizations, and societies. There are a few things that we *can* see affecting managers and organization. We also see some trends that will impact organizations, managers, and societies.

Managers

1. Will no longer be able to restrict the flow of corporate information. The Internet allows wide access to corporate information.
2. Will need to know how and when to direct global workforces and resources in order to compete effectively in a global economy.
3. Will need to learn how to work with culturally diverse virtual worldwide teams.
4. Will need to be technology savvy. It won't be required that managers are necessarily technical; however, they must know enough to understand technological trends and how these trends impact their businesses.
5. Will be held more accountable than their predecessors for their decisions because information about their decisions are accessible by employees and shareholders.
6. Will need to find creative ways to motivate workers in remote areas of the world.
7. Must be able to instill the vision and mission of their organizations to a globally diverse virtual workforce.

8. Must provide better corporate environments and rewards than their competitors in order to retain employees.

Organizations

1. Must be able to speed their products to market before their competition.
2. Must be able to compete globally.
3. Must adjust to the fact that hierarchical management structures are being collapsed by the flow of information and the need to empower workers.
4. Must compete with companies that may have less-expensive overhead and labor costs.
5. Must prepare for disruptive technologies that might upset their businesses.
6. Must create ways to focus their organizations on pleasing their customers.
7. Must compete globally for trained information technology workers.

Trends

1. Wages for "knowledge workers" will continue to rise until such time as information technology becomes a commodity.
2. The gap between rich and poor people and countries will widen as knowledge and speed to market increases.
3. Customers will find it easier to buy products and services as competition increases.
4. Creating new brands and achieving brand loyalty will be quite difficult in the Digital Age.
5. Costs will continue to decline for computer-related products and services as the industry matures.
6. The amount of people using the Internet worldwide will continue to increase.

7. Information technology is enabling businesses to enter the global marketplace.

8. Electronic commerce will continue to increase for consumers, industries, and governments.

9. Governments will continue and may very well succeed in legislating how the Internet will be used.

10. Entire workforces will require retraining or face low wages if they cannot contribute to the digital economy.

11. Business to business (B2B) commerce will continue to grow.

B2B COMMERCE: THE MAKING OF GLOBAL MONOPOLIES?

I would like to pause for a moment and share something that gravely concerns me about the potential dangers of B2B commerce. B2B refers to nothing more than businesses doing business with other businesses. Companies can and are getting together to see if they can create efficiencies and reduce their costs. This practice of course is basic for any company doing any business. However, major companies within industries such as manufacturing, chemicals, and pharmaceuticals are forming massive, powerful purchasing entities.

For example, the major automobile manufacturers have subscribed to an entity called Covisint. As I understand Covisint, it concentrates on providing savings to the manufacturers through managing the supply chain of products, such as metal for the manufacturers. On the surface this appears to be a good idea. What concerns me is that in order for suppliers to play in this new enterprise, they will be forced to lower their prices to the point where they would go out of business. This again is nothing new in business; however, what *is* new is the speed by which businesses could fail and the scope and gravity of failures. In other words, what concerns me is if the large manufacturers get together as it appears they are, and combine their requirements for all the steel they need under one or a few purchase orders, there would be but a few suppliers who would even qualify to bid. It is conceivable in my mind that entire economies could be financially depressed. According to the information contained in Covisint's Web site, "Internet technology is not about incremental improvements; e-business is a fundamental redesign of the enterprise" (January 15, 2001).

I bring this issue up because as a manager you may very well find yourself in the middle of having to make critical decisions when it comes to B2B commerce. You need to be aware of the possible ramifications for every organization involved. I see B2B commerce as potentially having as severe an impact on economies as disruptive technologies have on industries and companies.

In his best selling book *The Innovator's Dilemma*, Clayton Christensen describes how disruptive technologies hurt even well-managed companies. Disruptive technologies are those that usually emerge in a marketplace without much fanfare but significantly change an industry; not unlike the arrival of B2B commerce. Christensen sites the desktop copiers versus the large multiuser copiers and the steel minimills versus the large plants as examples of what happens to well-managed, customer-focused organizations. "Hence, most companies with a practiced discipline of listening to their best customers and identifying new products that promise greater profitability and growth are rarely able to build a case for investing in disruptive technologies until it is too late" (p. xvii). In the case of B2B commerce, if large blocks of purchasing power decide not to add a supplier such as the Brazilian rubber industry to its suppliers, the Brazilian rubber industry would be devastated with no time to respond or recover.

CONCLUDING REMARKS

It is my sincere hope that this book has reinforced your existing understanding of how organizations achieve superior results. Or it has provided you with new knowledge, understanding, and direction. As you progress throughout your management career, remember that as a manager you *must truly care* about and for your employees. Truly caring about people is the most important attribute of superior managers.

In caring for your employees you will naturally recognize that the well-being and motivation of the workforce is critical to the success of the organization. You must pay particular attention to employees as human beings having the same wants, needs, and desires as yourself. If you find yourself in an organizational culture that does not value and care for its employees, the organization is destined for failure.

Employees will determine how successful the organization will be in a competitive environment. The reason is simple. *In a competitive environment the difference between winning and losing is service.* Keep in mind that service is defined by what the customer receives from the organization. Customers not only receive products and services, they also receive impressions of the organization. The most desirable impression organizations want to deliver is quality service.

In nearly every organization *employees, not managers, render service.* As much as some managers think they provide the service, in fact it is the subordinates who render most of the service, products, and impressions to customers. Whenever I spoke to a group of CEOs I would ask them how long their companies could survive without them. Most agreed for at least 30 days. They would also agree that things would come to a screeching halt if their administrative staff, maintenance staff, receptionists, payroll clerks, or the cleaning crew decided not to come to work for 30 days. Employees run the organization.

Some managers have the mistaken idea that the higher they rise in the ranks they are more responsible for providing customer service. In actuality, the opposite is true. *The higher one goes up in management the less one has to do with the satisfaction of the customer.* We live in a time when customers expect good service, but "good" is not good enough any more. The organizations that consistently exceed their customers' expectations will be rewarded with loyalty, growth, and profit. The only way this can happen is through the workforce.

Many if not most of the managers reading this book face a daunting task. The task is to change the cultures of their organizations. Take heart! If top management truly wishes to transform itself into a superior customer service organization it can be done.

As this book comes to an end I must share a story with you. I got in the habit of ending my speeches with this story. You might be interested in knowing that over the years I calculate those audiences to add to over 150,000 managers. It brought nine out of ten audiences to their feet. As the story goes, there was a Catholic nun who had dedicated her life to teaching at a Midwestern high school. The year she was to retire the school principal asked that she deliver the commencement address to the graduating seniors. She accepted humbly. When the big day came she stepped to the podium, looked out over the gathering of students, friends, and proud families and said. "I promise that this will be the most popular commencement speech in the history of the school because it will be the shortest." The crowd cheered loudly. She then went on to say that in all her years of prayer and teaching she was convinced that "people did not care about how much that you and I know, they care about how much you and I care." I hope as you manage that you think about what the nun said.

Superior customer service organizations have clearly defined missions. They are great at communicating with their workforces. Their senior management truly cares and respects their employees. Their behavior is modeled throughout their organizations. The culture of their organization is focused on exceeding customer expectations. They celebrate successes and eliminate fear from the workplace.

TAKE CARE OF YOUR PEOPLE!

In the words of Walt Disney, "Take care of your people, your people will take care of the customers and the money will take care of itself." And while you are at it, take care of yourself. Good Luck!

Bibliography

Albrecht Karl and Ron Zemke. *Service America!* New York: Warner Books, Inc., 1985.

American Heritage Dictionary, Second College Edition. Boston: Houghton Mifflin Company, 1985.

Barnard, Chester I. *Functions of the Executive*. Cambridge, MA: Harvard University Press, 1938.

Blanchard, Kenneth D. and Spencer Johnson. *The One-Minute Manager*. New York: Berkley Books, 1981.

Butters, Patrick. "Andrew Carnegie: Ruthless and Rich." *Washington Post*, January 19, 1977.

Christensen, Clayton M. *The Innovator's Dilemma: When New Technologies Cause Great Firms to Fail*. Boston: Harvard Business School Press, 1997.

Chronicle of America. Mount Kisco, NY: Chronicle Publications, 1989.

Collins, James C. and Jerry I. Porras. *Built to Last: Successful Habits of Visionary Companies*. New York: HarperBusiness, 1994.

Cribbin, James J. *Leadership: Strategies for Organizational Effectiveness*. New York: Amacom, 1981.

Dertouzos, Michael. *What Will Be: How the New World of Information Will Change Our Lives*. New York: HarperCollins, 1997.

Drucker, Peter. "Sage Advice." *Business 2.0.* San Francisco: Imagine Media, Inc., August 22, 2000.

Follett, Mary Parker. "Power" (1925) in *Dynamic Administration, The Collected Papers of Mary Parker Follett*, Henry C. Metcaff and L. Urwick, eds. New York: Harper, 1942.

Forbes Magazine. "Peter Drucker," October 5, 1998.

Forbes, 70th Anniversary Issue, Vol. 140, Number 1, July 13, 1987.

Freiberg, Kevin and Jackie. *NUTS! Southwest Airlines' Crazy Recipe for Business and Personal Success.* New York: Broadway Books, 1996.

Friedman, Thomas L. *The Lexus and the Olive Tree: Understanding Globalization.* New York: Farrar, Straus and Giroux, 1999.

Gabor, Andrea. *The Man Who Discovered Quality: How W. Edwards Deming Brought the Quality Revolution to America—The Stories of Ford, Xerox, and GM.* New York: Random House, Inc., 1990.

Goodman, Ted, ed. *The Forbes Book of Business Quotations: 14,173 Thoughts on the Business of Life.* New York: Black Dog & Leventhal Publishers, Inc., 1997.

Hamel, Gary and C.K. Prahalad. *Competeing for the Future.* Boston: Harvard Business School Press, 1994.

Hammer, Michael and James Champy. *Reengineering the Corporation: A Manifesto for Business Revolution.* New York: HarperCollins, 1993.

Harvard Business Review. "75 Years of Management Ideas and Practice," September–October 1997.

Herzberg, Frederick. "One More Time: How Do You Motivate Employees?" *Harvard Business Review*, January–February 1968.

Heyel, Carl, ed. *The Encyclopedia of Management*, 2nd ed. New York: Van Nostrand Reinhold Company, 1973.

Jones, LeRoi. *The New York Public Book Library, Book of 20th Century American Quotes.* Stonesong Press, Inc., and the New York Public Library. New York: Warner Books, Inc., 1992.

Katz, Robert. "Skills of an Effective Administrator," *Harvard Business Review*, January–February (reissued September–October 1974).

Love, John L. *McDonald's Behind the Arches*. New York: Bantam Books, Inc,. 1986.

Lowe, Janet. *Jack Welch Speaks: Wisdom form the World's Greatest Business Leader*. New York: John Wiley & Sons, Inc., 1998.

Marriott, J.W. Jr. and Kathi Ann Brown. *The Spirit to Serve— Marriott's Way*. New York: HarperBusiness, 1997.

Maslow, A.H. "A Theory of Human Motivation." *Psychology Review*, 50, 1943.

McGregor, Douglas. *The Human Side of Enterprise*. New York: McGraw-Hill, 1959.

Moseley, Leonard. *The Real Walt Disney*. London: Futura Publications, 1987.

Myhrvold, Nathan and Peter Rinearson. *Bill Gates: The Road Ahead*. New York: Viking Penguin, 1995.

Naisbitt, John. *Preparing Now for the Next Decade: A Preview of Emerging Trends*. John Naisbitt's Trend Letter, Washington, D.C., 1989.

Nelson, Emily and Evan Ramstad. "Hershey's Biggest Dud Has Turned Out To Be Its New Technology," *Wall Street Journal*, October 29, 1999.

Nightingale, Earl. *Earl Nightingale's Greatest Discovery*. New York: Dodd, Mead & Company, 1987.

Oliver, Thomas. *The Real Coke, The Real Story*. New York: Penguin Books, 1986.

Pearlstein, Steven. "Reengineering Management." *Washington Post*, January 29, 1995.

Peters, Thomas J. and Robert H. Waterman, Jr. *In Search of Excellence: Lessons from America's Best-Run Companies*. New York: Harper & Row, 1982.

Peters and Waterman. Film Interview based on the book *In Search of Excellence*. Produced by John Nathen and Sam Tyler Productions, n.d.

Senge, Peter M. *The Fifth Discipline: The Art and Practice of the Learning Organization*. New York: Doubleday, 1990.

Sewell, Carl. *Customers for Life: How to Turn That One-Time Buyer into a Lifetime Customer*. New York: Pocket Books, 1990.

Tapscott, Don. *The Digital Economy: Promises and Peril in the Age of Networked Intelligence*. New York: McGraw-Hill, 1996.

Taylor, Frederick W. *The Principles of Scientific Management*. New York: Harper & Bros., 1911.

Thomas, Bob. *Walt Disney, An American Original*. New York: Simon & Schuster, 1976.

Thurow, Lester. *Head to Head, The Coming Economic Battle Among Japan, Europe and America*. New York: William Morrow and Company, 1992.

Walton, Sam with John Huey. *Sam Walton, Made in America: My Story*. New York: Bantam Books, 1993.

Watson, Thomas J. Jr. and Peter Petre. *Father, Son & Co.: My Life at IBM and Beyond*. New York: Bantam Books, 1990.

Index

Computer revolution, 18. *See also* Information age
Consumer movement, 17
Covisint, 149–50
Culture, corporate, 47–52, 115–26; attitudes toward employees in, 115–16; communication system and, 84–85, 94; creation of, 1–3; definition of, 47; and employee training and orientation, 74, 75–76; and leading by example, 49–50, 52; and management selection, 63–64; and mission implementation, 32–33; orientation programs and, 75–76; and recognition and rewards, 116–21; time management and, 98–99; training programs and, 74–76
Customer: loyalty, motivated employees and, 36; position, in organizational structure, 40, 43–44
Customer experiences: analysis of, 106–12; and employee motivation, 106, 110; operational systems and, 110–12
Customer service organizations, 20; basic premise of, 17, 28; competition and, 17; defining mission in, 131; effective communication in, 83–87, 134–35; emotion and

compassion in, 64; institutionalized recognition practices in, 116–21; organizational structure and, 43–44; politics and, 140–41; recognition of employees in, 137; respect for employees in, 132–33; senior managers' attitudes in, 36, 43; staff training in, 136; time management in, 97–102. *See also* EDS; Walt Disney World
Customers for Life (Sewell), 86, 111

Davis, Tom, 141
De Feather, Emile, 83
Delacroix, Eugene, 97
Deming, W. Edwards, 73
Dertouzos, Michael, 146–47
Disney, Walt, 48, 58, 100–101, 131, 152. *See also* Walt Disney World
Divisional accounting, 13
Drucker, Peter F., 1, 39

EDS, 119, 130; Barcelona Olympics marketing project, 138; Pavilion project, 131–40; World Congress on Information Technology and, 139–40
Educational system, U.S., 73–74
Eisner, Michael, 67

About the Author

JIM POISANT is President/CEO of Poisant International, LLC, a management consulting firm specializing in senior-level international congresses and summits that focus on Information Technology. In addition, Dr. Poisant is Associate Visiting Professor at the School of Management at George Mason University and was the founding first manager of Business Seminars for the Walt Disney Co.